Romance of the Raga

Romance of the Raga

Vijaya Moorthy

ABHINAV PUBLICATIONS

abhinav publications

Plate 18 (on page 2). Raga Sri, Mughal.

Plate XXXIX. Ektara (Gourd and Bamboo), West Bengal.

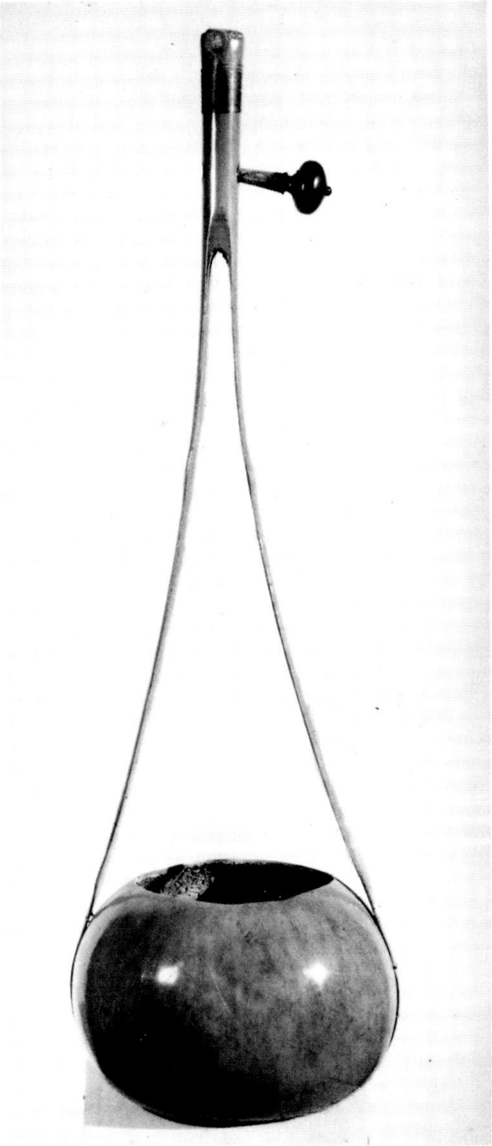

First published in India 2001

Publishers
Shakti Malik
Abhinav Publications
E-37 Hauz Khas
New Delhi-110016 (INDIA)
Phones: 6566387, 6562784, 6524658
Fax: 91-11-6857009
e-mail: shakti@nde.vsnl.net.in
Website: http://www.abhinavexports.com

ISBN 81-7017-382-5

Phototypesetting and Processing by
Tara Chand Sons
C-139, Mansarovar Garden, New Delhi

Printed at
D.K. Fine Art Press Pvt. Ltd.
Ashok Vihar, Delhi

For
Sai Baba of Shirdi

"Oh Supreme Sadguru,
boundless is your power
and marvellous your deeds!
You are the ship transporting
the ignorant
across the Ocean of Life."

—The Song of Das Ganu

Plate 14. Rāgaputra Sarang, Malwa, Central India.

Plate 2. Ruima Veena, South India.

Contents

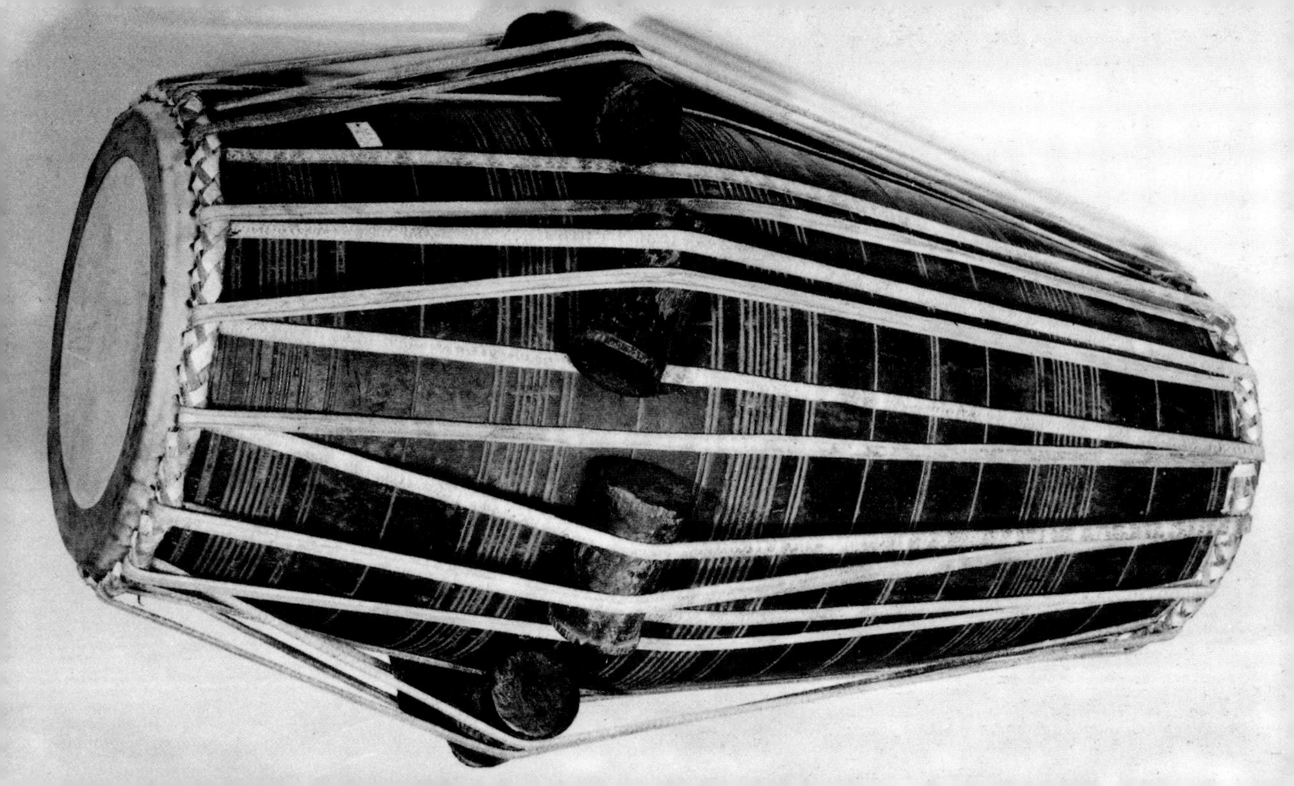

Acknowledgement

Gratitude is expressed to the National Museum, New Delhi for according permission to publish the Colour Illustrations at Plates 1 to 20 and Black and White Illustrations at Plates I to XL, from their collection.

Vijaya Moorthy

Plate XXXII. Pakhawaj, Rampur, Uttar Pradesh.

Foreword

The human mind is an enigma, while the potential for creative expression by the intellect is indeed unlimited and unfathomable!

The rich heritage of the Indian Musical Tradition is based on the belief that Sound is God and *Nada Brahma* or Intelligible Sound is the manifestation of the fusion of the physical breath with the fire of the intellect. Thus Indian Classical Music is viewed as a spiritual discipline that elevates one's Inner Self to the heights of Divinity and Self-Realisation.

The *Raga* is one such medium—a medium that transcends, with a drift so powerful well beyond the gulf of time! The *Raga* when faithfully rendered enables both the performer and the listener to share most vividly the intimate thoughts, innermost feelings, sentiments and emotions experienced by the revered musicians, composers and performers.

As a unique form of musical expression, once understood, it becomes well and truly a manifestation of the nuances, aesthetic perceptions and sensibilities of the musician, while at the same time enthralling the listener for having inculcated within himself the capacity to appreciate and enjoy the experience.

Instantly evocative, articulate and poignant, great renderings in Indian Classical Music could be diverse and varied in expression—contemplative and meditative like a Prayer; appealing, tantalizing and yet elusive like a Romance; mysterious and obscure like a Shrouded Sculptural Masterpiece, waiting to be unveiled; or grand, imposing and with regality and splendour, like a Caparisoned Elephant! Thus whatever be the qualities or attributes of the musical composition, an appreciation of the classical tradition of Indian Music could elevate the listener to almost unimaginable heights of ecstasy and bliss. Such is the multi-faceted capability inherent in this rich tradition and form of creative and artistic rendering—a system based on unity within diversity, scientific methodology, evolution, fusion, continuity and above all Synthesis!

Tone merged with note, theme fused with melody and rhythm with tempo, the true character of classical music of India possesses the qualities of elegance, intricate yet subtle ornamentation and above all spirit.

Plate 19. Raga Malkaunsa, Uniara, Rajasthan.

In this book, an attempt has been made to outline the evolution, historical traditions, perspectives, distinct styles and the sheer range and variety of musical instruments, with a view to delineate the qualities mentioned above, with the objective of providing the reader a better understanding and appreciation of Indian Classical Music.

Romance and mystery are so closely interwoven into the fabric of this art form that I hope this work would enable one to first unravel and thereafter explore a great tradition beyond the horizon.

New Delhi **S.N. Gulati**
12th December, 1996

Preface

Several weighty and authoritative documents and works on the subject of Indian Classical Music and its priceless tradition have been authored by renowned musicologists, scholars and experts. This work can, at best, be viewed as an outline, or better still, as a glimpse of the great historical tradition inherited by us, the various techniques and styles in presentation and a reference to the shapers of the musical destiny.

The basic purpose of this work is to enable an enthusiast to acquire the required degree of understanding which in turn could constitute the foundation to facilitate a better appreciation of the Classical Tradition of Indian Music.

In the interest of clarity and visual appreciation of the contents of this book, illustrations have been featured at places considered suitable. Further, a Glossary of essential terminology has been appended for easy reference.

A large number of books have been consulted. Some of these have been mentioned at the end of the volume. This book includes a glossary of musical terms, a select bibliography and a select discography.

My sincere gratitude to The National Museum, New Delhi, for their permission to reproduce the Plates on Indian Miniatures and Musical Instruments, from their rich collection. In the absence of these illustrations, depiction and portrayal of the sheer variety and range, as also the all-important aspect of the thematic content of the *Raga*, would have been difficult to project!

Hyderabad
18th December, 1996

Vijaya Moorthy

Plate 6. Mira, North India.

Plate 16. Ragini Vasanta, Mewar, Rajasthan. →

॥रागणीवसंत॥श्रीरागरीरागणी

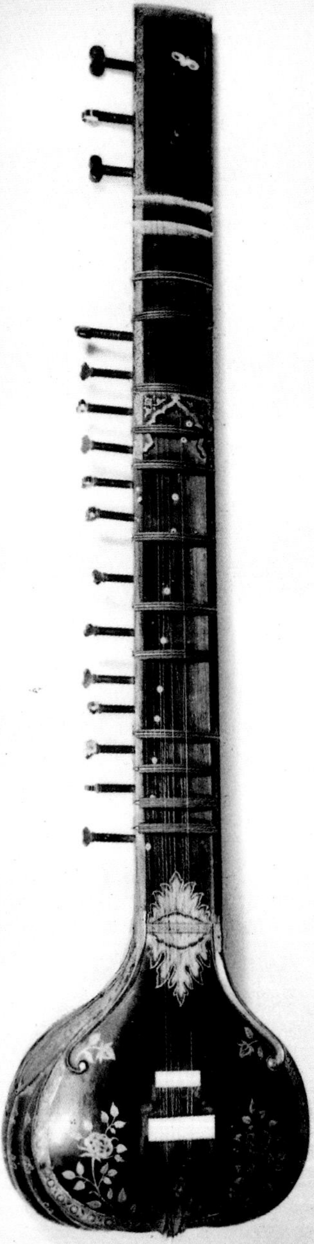

CHAPTER I

Indian Classical Music— A Historical Perspective

"Many are the great souls;
to them all my salutations."

—Saint Tyagaraja

The traditions of Indian classical music, though rooted in antiquity and at times intertwined with legend and mythology, are only seemingly without a beginning. Contemporary Indian classical music undoubtedly has its roots in ancient Indian music, although it is believed to have acquired its present form only after the 14th century A.D.

Legend has it that the origins of this divine art are ascribed to the Trinity —*Brahma* the Creator, *Vishnu* the Preserver and *Shiva* the Destroyer. According to mythology, the everlasting rhythm of life and death in the Universe is symbolised by the Cosmic Dance or *Tandava* of *Shiva.*

However while it is indeed difficult to sift and sieve legend from history, as far as the origins of Ancient Indian music are concerned, it is now believed that the *Vedas* are the link in the ocean of continuity, although historically speaking, the evolution of music in India can be traced way back to at least 2000 B.C. Recent excavations have also revealed that the people of the Indus Valley Civilisation, probably *pre-Aryan,* were skilled in the playing of flutes and primitive drums.

From literary sources it is now well known that *Aryans* living in India before the 1st century B.C. chanted *Mantras* and recited hymns while performing religious ceremonies. *Vedic* literature also contains references to musical instruments and the chants of the *Samaveda,* collectively referred to as the *Samagana,* are believed to be the root of Indian classical music.

In early *Vedic* music, the hymns centred around the two notes—*Udatta* or "raised" note and the *Anudatta* or "unraised" note. Gradually the *Svarita* or "sounded" note was added. In the *Rikpratisakhya,* a musical treatise of the 4th century B.C., names are given to each of these notes.

The *Vedic* hymns, recited later on, extended to seven different notes and ultimately the complete *Saptaka* of seven notes or *Swaras* was formulated.

← Plate XI. Sitar, Rajasthan.

Indian musical theory is expounded in considerable detail in the *Natyashastra*. A work attributed to the Sage *Bharata*, it is among the oldest and most important treatises on the performing arts. Believed to have been written around the 2nd century A.D., it is also perhaps the earliest text on the art of dramatics, amongst which music has been included. Although it is now established that the musical system of Ancient India, as described therein, varied considerably from that of today and the concept of *Raga* as a technical term was not mentioned, researches have revealed that music based on the principle of *Moorchana*, that is the shifting of the tonic note or scale progressions in descending motion from the fundamental notes, was in existence.

In fact, the first mention of *Raga* is stated to occur in *Brihaddeshi* (*brihad*: great, *deshi*: regional, secular) by *Matanga* (c. 5th century A.D.). *Matanga* had also stipulated that a *Raga* must contain at least five *Swaras* in both the ascending and descending scales.

Later the concept was elaborated upon in *Sarangadeva's Sangitaratnakara* (first half of the 13th century A.D.). Written at the court of a *Yadava* king in the Deccan, by *Sarangadeva*, an emigrant from *Kashmir*, shortly before the Muslim conquest, the work is characterised by the absence of Muslim influence on Indian music, which came to be later. It also indicates that *Ragas* had proliferated considerably in number, for *Sarangadeva* refers to two hundred and sixty-four of them. However, it is not possible to assess with precision as to how many of these were current, as the distinction between contemporary practice and antiquated theory was not adequately transparent. Interestingly, the *Sangitaratnakara* renders in considerable detail, descriptions of scales, *Ragas*, *Talas*, musical forms and diverse subjects. Of great significance is the fact that it is among the major pioneering works dealing with North and South Indian systems of Indian music. It is also contended by certain scholars that it was during this period that Indian music got bifurcated into the two distinct systems of *Hindustani* and *Karnatak* schools.

Music continued to flourish in the Deccan under the *Yadava* kings and to such an extent, that after the Muslim conquest led by the *Malik Kafur* (c. 1310 A.D.) several musicians and their Hindu preceptors were taken by the royal armies, to the North. The renowned poet *Amir Khusrau* at the court of *Ala-ud-din Khalji*, who was well versed both in Indian and Persian music, is full of praise for Indian music. *Khusrau*, a great innovator, enriched Indian music and also increased the repertoire of Indian instruments. As an astute political adviser, he was a mentor and adviser to eleven Rulers of Delhi, particularly of the *Khalji* Dynasty. *Khusrau* was a prolific Persian scholar and versatile *Sufi* who loved *Brij Bhasa* and *Sanskrit*, composed *Quals* (Muslim devotional songs) and *Taranas* and above all attempted to 'synthesise' *Persian* and *Brij*. However while the origin of the musical form *Khyal* and the invention of the *Sitar* are attributed to him, he himself does not mention the fact.

With the advent of Muslims, development of music continued with great gusto and gathered considerable momentum through the *Sufi* Movement. Sufi mysticism, a philosophy of Islam that arose in the tenth century, was most popular in Persia and through its doctrines viewed music as a medium of devotion and God realisation, in many ways, akin to the concept of *Bhakti*. The universality of the precepts of *Sufism* and *Bhakti* arises from the fundamental premise—Oneness of the Supreme Being. Spiritual enlightenment and upliftment coupled with Universal love constitute the basis for devotion.

Almost concurrently, in the Tamil land, the *Vaishnavite Alvars* decried social bifurcations and injustice and sang in praise of devotion and surrender to the Supreme Being. The teachings of *Ramanujam* (12th-13th century A.D.), based on the precepts of *Bhakti*, had an enormous impact on social attitudes and beliefs. Similarly the influence of *Madhava* (13th century A.D.) and his followers resulted in the composition of soul-stirring songs. *Sri Purandara dasa* was amongst the greatest of the saints who was not only a pioneering musician but also one of the renowned composers of *Karnatak* music.

Yet another immortal landmark in the history of Indian music is the *Sanskrit* poem *Gita Govinda*, written by *Jayadeva* (c. 12th century). There is some doubt regarding the place of his birth. It is believed that *Jayadeva* was born at *Kinduhilvam* (also called *Kenduli*) on the northern bank of the River *Ajaya*, in *Orissa*. *Gita Govinda*, a monumental work, is a *Sringara Mahakavya* in 12 *Sargas*, written in chaste *Sanskrit*. Further, it is not only a magnificient musical composition, but also a literary masterpiece, which in turn inspired painting, dance and mystic adoration of the finest order. It consists of 24 songs, each song in turn containing 8 *Charanas* and hence the name *Ashtapadi*. The *Ashtapadi* hymns, rich in description, contain vivid portrayals of various stuations, apart from being beautiful examples of flowery metrical *Sahityas*. They belong to the realm of sacred music and are frequently rendered at concerts of art music as well. In fact the *Gita Govinda* is often described as the nucleus which provided the inspiration for the development of classical opera and dance drama, a few centuries later. *Jayadeva* was a devout *Bhakta* (devotee) of *Lord Krishna*. The exclusion by him of *Lord Krishna* from his *Dasavtaras* indicates that he revered and regarded *Lord Krishna* as *Parabrahma*.

Worship of *Lord Krishna* in the *Nayaka Nayaki Bhava* (*Madhura Bhava* approach to the Supreme Being) found considerable following. *Jiva Brahma Aikya Vedanta Rahasya* or the Union of the individual soul with the Universal Soul is in brief the theme and essence of *Gita Govinda*. *Radha* (*Nayaki* or *Jivatma*), *Krishna* (*Nayaka* or the *Paramatma*) and *Sakhi* (the friend or preceptor who leads the devotee on to the path of *Mukti* or liberation) are among the prominent characters in the book. The mutual love of *Radha* and *Krishna*, intense but delicate, is truly representative of the concept of *Madhura Bhakti*, the essence of *Vaishnavite* adoration.

Plate 1. Ganesh and Saraswati, Sikh Style, Punjab.

Though *Jayadeva* refers to *Raga* and *Tala* for each *Ashtapadi*, the original mode of rendering is not known. Sir William Jones , the famous Indologist, recounts his difficulties in tracing the original music of the *Ashtapadi* Hymns thus:

"When I first read the songs of Jayadeva, who has prefaced to each the name of the mode in which it was to be sung, I had hopes of procuring the original music; but the Pandits of the South referred me to those of the West, and the Brahmans of the West would have sent me to those of the North , while they of Nepal and Kashmir declared that they had no ancient music but imagined that the notes of 'Gita Govinda' must exist, if anywhere , where the poet was born."

Plate 3. Hazrat Nizamuddin Aulia and Amir Khusrau, Deccan, Hyderabad.

Sir William Jones had also published a translation of portions of the *Gita Govinda* in "Asiatic Researches", Volume III, 1799. The *Gita Govinda* was also translated into English by Sir Edwin Arnold and published under the title "The Indian Song of Songs".

Thus the wave of Bhakti engulfed the entire sub-continent and became an irresistible force in the religious and musical life of the country. Among the well-known greatest minstrels of the time were *Sankar Dev* of *Assam, Krishna Chaitanya* of *Bengal, Mira Bai, Tulsi Das, Kabir, Sur Das* and *Tukaram,* who composed *Bhajans* and *Abhangs* along with the Sufis, thereby giving expression to their ardent and intense spiritual experiences through the medium of the language of music.

The intensity of devotion and spiritual expression through the medium of music is amply demonstrated by the following narration. The profundity of insight of *Sadguru Sai Baba of Shirdi,* to whom this work is dedicated in all humility, is well known to his devotees. Among the artists patronised by *Baba,* was *Khansahib Abdul Karim Khan.* In 1914, to the accompaniment of various instruments, *Khansahib* rendered in *Raga Piloo "hechi dana dega deva",* an *Abhang* composed by *Tukaram.* Such was the intensity of devotion that *Baba,* with his eyes closed, listened in rapt attention. When the *Abhang* was over, *Baba* opened his eyes and exclaimed: *"Ah, how well he sang! Such is his intensity in praying that one feels like granting his prayer!" Khansahib* had acquainted himself with the favourite *Bhajans* and *Abhangs* of *Baba* and sang "*Aur nahi kachchu kamki main bharose apne Ramki*" in *Raga Darbari Kannada.* He then sang the *Abhang* composed by *Tukaram* "*Je ne ranjale ganjale tyasi mhane jo apule"* and then proceeded to render *"is a tana dhanaki kaun badhai"* , a *Doha* of *Kabir* in *Raga Jogia.*

Reverting to the chronological narration of the evolution of Indian classical music, the regime of *Sultan Mohammed Bin Tughlak* (1325-1351 A.D.) who patronised music on a grand scale, is significant. From the accounts of *Ibn Batuta* the Sultan is reported to have had as many as 1,200 musicians at his court in addition to 1,000 slave musicians.

With the continued extension of royal patronage, the musical treatise *Sangitasiromani* was dedicated to *Ibrahim Shah Sharqui* of *Jaunpur* in 1428 A.D. while the *Sultan Zain-ul-Abidin* of *Kashmir* is credited with the composition of a treatise on music.

In the years following, *Raja Man Singh Tomar* of *Gwalior* (1486-1516 A.D.) rejuvenated the *Dhruvapad* (also popularly referred to as *Dhrupad*) style. Derived from the term *Dhruva,* "definite or fixed" and *pada* "word", it is believed to have its roots in the *Prabandha Geets,* which in turn are based on the *Sama Gana* of the *Vedas.* Reputed to be amongst the oldest forms of Indian classical music, this style received considerable impetus during the reign of *Raja Man Singh Tomar.* Several compositions in this style are also attributed to *Mian Tansen,* the jewel at the Court of *Emperor*

Akbar. Raja Man Singh was also responsible for the compilation of a progressive treatise in Hindi, named *Man Kautuhal* (Curiosities of Man). This notable work is said to contain the records of the proceedings of a great conference of musical experts, assembled at the behest of the *Raja*. It also incorporates many of the innovations introduced since the time of *Amir Khusrau*. According to *Sir W. Ousley* (Anecdotes of Indian Music), the treatise was translated into Persian by *Faquir Ullah*. In the words of *Cunningham* (Archaeological Survey of India Reports, Volume II, 1862), the *Raja* was a *"proficient composer, as well as a munificient patron, and many of his compositions still survive to justify the esteem in which they are held by his contemporaries. He was specially fond of the sankirna ragas, or mixed modes of which no less than four specimens are named after his favourite Gujarni (Guzerati) queen, Mrganena (Mrga-nayana) or the "fawn-eyed". These are Gujari, Bahul Gujari, Mal-Gujari, and Mangal Gujari."* *Abul Fazl* in *Ain-i-Akbari* has further corroborated the patronage extended by the *Raja* by stating that three of *Raja Man's* musicians: *Naik, Nukshoo* and *Bhanau* formed a collection of songs which found popular appeal.

Husayn Shah Sharqui, a contemporary of *Raja Man Singh*, is credited with the introduction of the *Khyal* form of singing. *Khyal* denotes 'thought' or 'imagination' and this unique and versatile form of vocal rendering is characterised by delicately ornamented phrases and freedom to improvise, subject of course to the conventions that determine the boundaries, form and structure of the *Raga*.

During the regime of the *Lodi* Dynasty, the reign of *Sultan Sikandar Lodi* of Delhi (1489-1517 A.D.) is significant. The *Sultan* was a great poet, who was deeply interested in music and the first treatise on Indian music in Persian, the *Lahjat-i-Sikandar Shahi*, was written under his patronage. Interestingly this work was based on the existing Sanskrit treatises thereby signifying the gradual and subtle synthesis emerging in the form of music evolving in the Northern part of India.

The reign of *Ibrahim Adil Shah II* of *Bijapur* of the Deccan (1580-1626 A.D.) is also of significance in the history of Indian music as there was an increasing interest in the theory of music and its association with *Rasa* or emotion, colour as also the visual representation of *Ragas*. Himself a renowned poet and musician, his reign characterises his liberal views and earnest attempts to integrate the elements of *Islamic* and *Hindu* philosophy. The *Kitab-i-Nauras* (*Nava Rasa* or nine emotions) contains a collection of his poems, intended to be sung in different *Ragas*

It was under the Mughal Emperors, *Akbar* (1555-1605 A.D.), *Jahangir* (1605-1627 A.D.) and *Shah Jahan* (1628-1658 A.D.), that the extension of royal patronage to music attained unprecedented heights and assumed extremely significant dimensions and proportions, more especially in the context of acceleration of the pace of refinement and evolution of the style and character of *Hindustani* classical music as it exists in its present form.

Plate 4. Gita-Govinda, Basohli, Pahari.

With the advent of *Akbar,* one of the most enthusiastic patrons of Indian culture in all its dimensions, Indian classical music approached a period of glory. Music was performed on a grand scale and according to *Abul Fazl Allami,* the orchestra which played in the gateway of the Royal Palace (*Naqqarakhana*) comprised more than sixty members. Further, while *Akbar* himself was a prolific composer according to the *Akbarnama,* the unquestionably towering and famous composer and musician *Miya Tansen,* who was the disciple of *Swami Haridas,* heralded an era of musical glory, under the patronage of the Emperor. Several *Ragas* bear his name, including *Miya Todi* and *Miya Malhar.* The *Dhrupad* style of singing gained further prominence. Interestingly, the majority of vocalists hailed from *Gwalior* while many of the instrumentalists were foreigners who came from as far as *Mashhad* and *Tabriz* in *Iran* and from *Herat* in modern *Afghanistan.*

At this stage, it would be appropriate to highlight the significant contribution of *Swami Haridas,* the mystic saint of *Brindavan,* who belonged to the tradition of *Madhura Bhakti* and whose musical genius has been immortalised through his *Vishnupadas, Dhrupads, Trivats* and *Ragamalas.* The *Haridasi* school of mysticism had many famous spiritual disciples including *Vitthala, Vipul, Viharin Deva* and *Krishna Das,* who fostered his tradition of devotional music, the essential feature of this tradition being its congregational approach. Thus groups of devotees came together and sang in praise of *Lord Krishna,* the Lord of *Brindavan.* In the *Brij* district, this congregation is referred to as *Samaj* and is similar to the *Sankeertan* of Bengal and *Bhajan Ghosti* of South India.

Though one of the greatest *Gurus* and musicians of his time, the Saint was amazingly indifferent to laurels and fame. His humility, greatness and proficiency as also the strength and resilience of the *Guru Shishya Parampara* (student and teacher relationship) are well described in the following episode. The story goes that while *Emperor Akbar* wanted to hear the music of *Swami Haridas,* it was impossible to bring the *Swami* to the royal court; and the *Ashram* (hermitage) was out of bounds. Therefore, *Tansen* thought of a ruse. *Akbar* would accompany *Tansen* to *Nidhuvan,* disguised as a *Tanboora* bearer. The two went as planned and the Emperor listened with rapt attention to the divine music of the *Swami.* On return to the Court, *Akbar* remarked to *Tansen,* "*How is it that with all your virtuosity, your music is so insipid compared to your guru's?*" *Tansen* replied, "*What else can it be: for I sing to the Emperor of this land but he sings to the Emperor of Creation.*" This episode is thus illustrative of the humility and egalitarian attitude of *Emperor Akbar,* the divinity of *Swami Haridas* and the devotion of his disciple, *Miya Tansen*!

Music continued to flourish during the reign of *Emperor Jahangir,* a great patron of arts and himself a skilled painter. *Bilas Khan,* the son of *Tansen,* was the principal musician at his court.

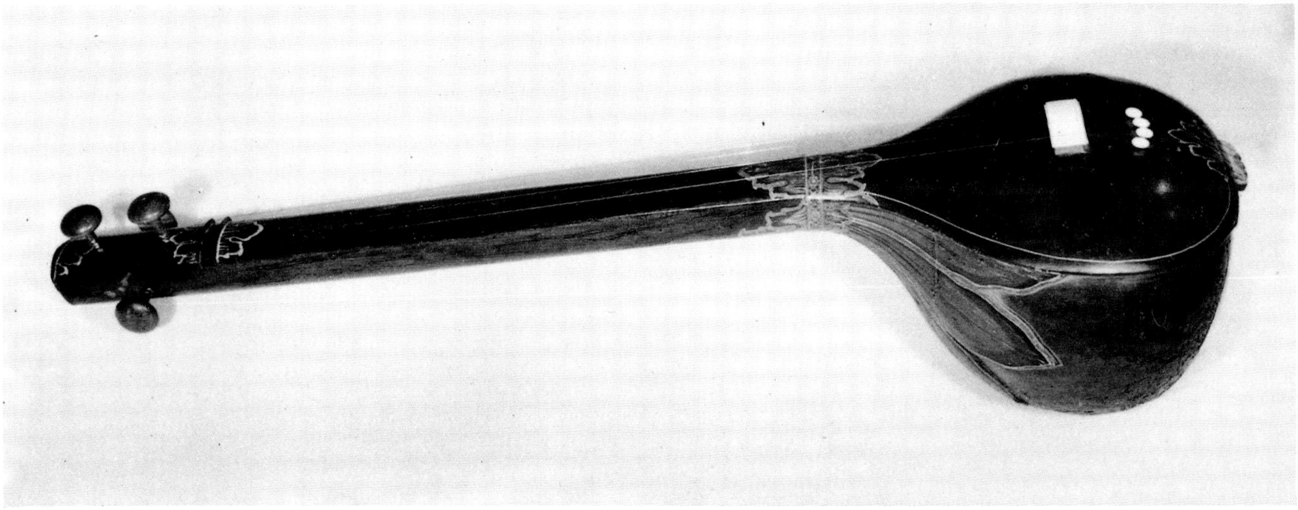

Plate II. Tambura, Mysore or Vijayanagaram (Near Waltair).

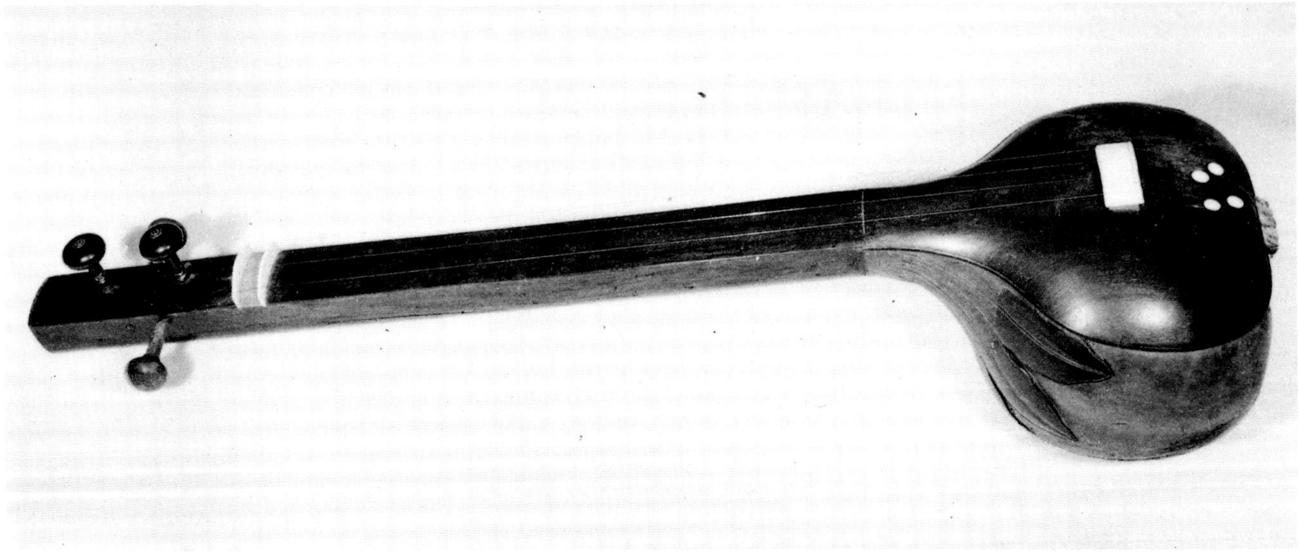

Plate III. Tanpura, Rajasthan.

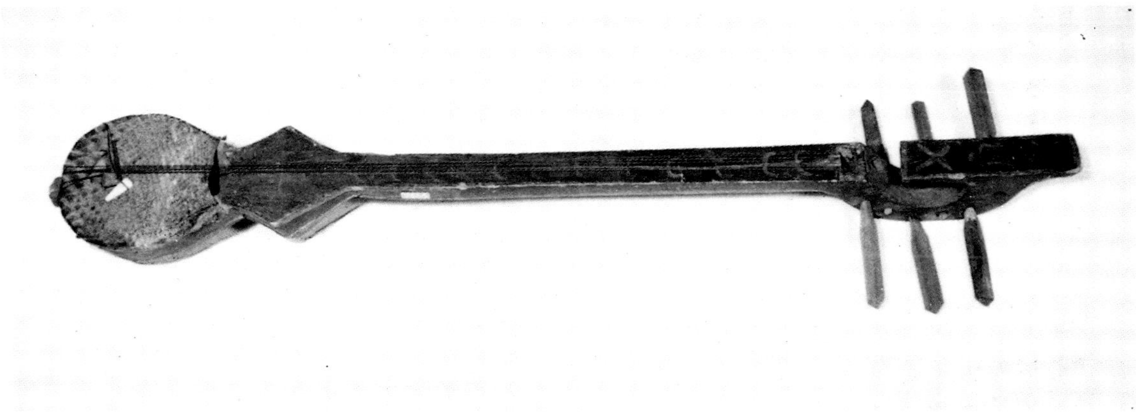

Plate I. Folk Instrument, Kalimpong, Darjeeling, North Bengal.

Music further attained unprecedented polish and grace during the reign of *Emperor Shah Jahan. Lal Khan,* pupil and son-in-law of *Bilas Khan,* continued relentlessly the tradition of *Miya Tansen.* A significant aspect during this period was the appreciable decrease in the influx of foreign musicians since the days of *Akbar.*

Meanwhile in the South, the 16th and 17th centuries were of tremendous significance in the history of Indian musical literature. The *Swaramelakalanidhi* of *Ramamatya,* a Minister of *Rama Raja,* Prince of *Vijayanagar,* focuses attention on the fact that the music of South India was evolving in its own way and acquiring a distinct identity and character. In fact one of the most important treatises on the *Karnatak* system was the *Caturdandiprakasika* of *Venkatamakhi,* written in 1660 A.D., in which the classification of *Ragas* in terms of 72 basic scales (*Mela Kartas*) was first advocated. According to the *Mela Karta* system, these *Ragas* correspond exactly to the 72 scales in the ascending and descending structures. It is surmised by some scholars that this changeover was due to *Iranian* influence, which brought in the concept of *Thata* (*Hindustani* word for *Mela*). However it is important to note that in the *Hindustani* system, the *Ragas* do not have the same structure as the *Thatas* on which they are based.

Around the same period several important treatises including the *Ragataringini* by *Locana Kavi* (date uncertain), the works of *Pundarika Vitthala* (end of 16th century A.D.) and *Sangitaparijata* by *Ahobala* (c. 1665 A.D.) had considerable

पातस्याहअकबर

Plate 5. Swami Haridas with Tansen and Emperor Akbar at Vrindavan, Kishengarh or Jaunpur.

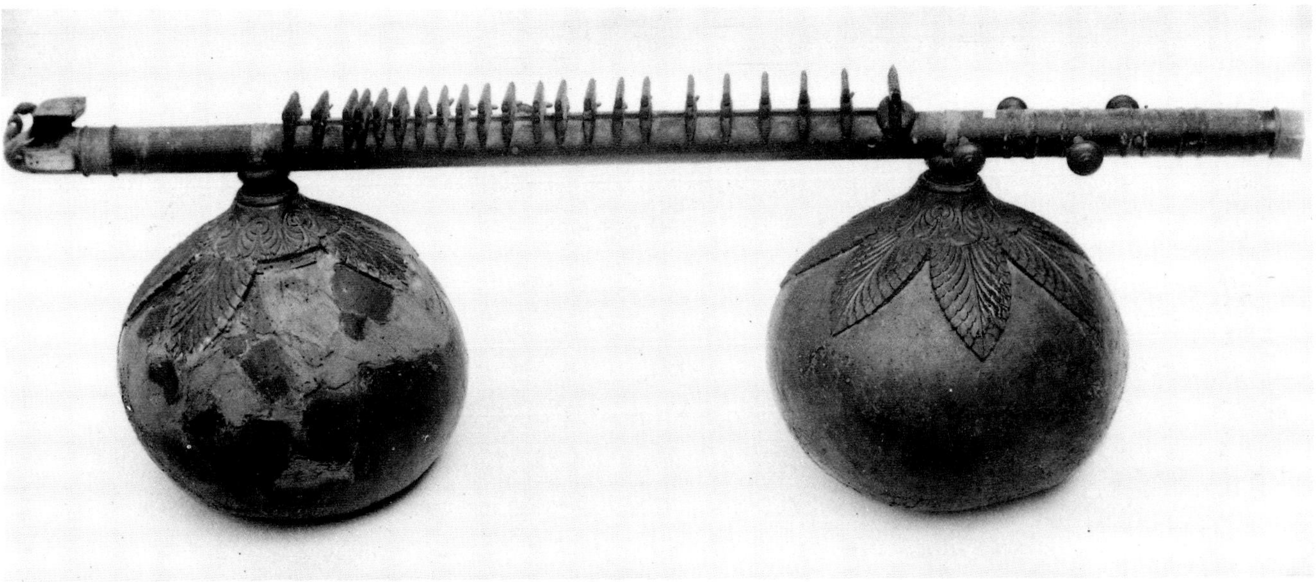

Plate V. Rudra Veena, of Late Raja Sri S.M. Tagore, 1840-1914, 19th Century A.D., North India..

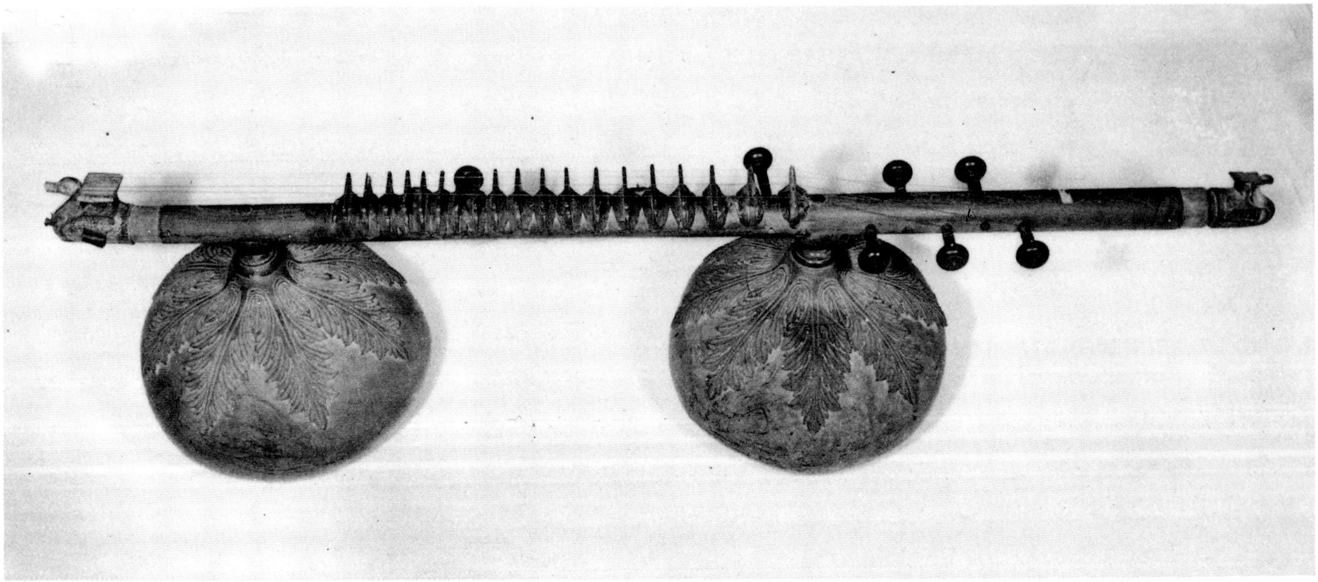

Plate VI. Saraswati Veena (Rudra Veena), Rajasthan, North India.

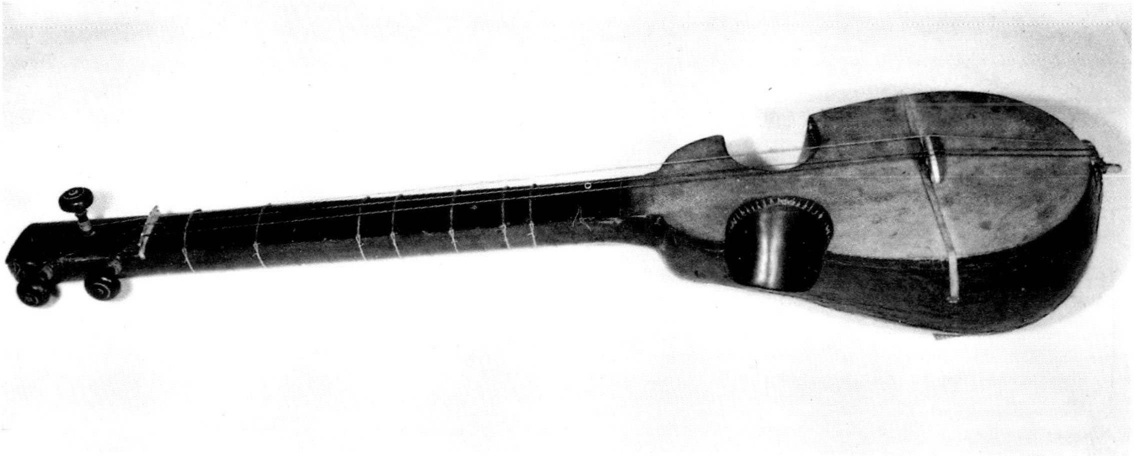

Plate IV. Mandra Bahar, Bengal.

bearing on the history of present day classical music. The *Ragavibodha* of *Somanath* (1609 A.D.) or the *Doctrine of Musical Modes,* a copy of which was discovered by *Sir William Jones,* consists of masterly couplets in the melodious metre called *Arya* and a minute description of different *Veenas* along with rules for playing on them.

The *Sangitadarpana* (1625 A.D.) of *Damodar Misra,* or the *Mirror of Modes,* wherein a list of 20 major *Ragas* has been enunciated, was written during the reign of *Shah Jahan.* The *Ragaranava* or *Sea of Passions* and the *Sabhavinoda* or *Delight of Assemblies* are also considered to be scriptures of practically equal value, on the development of Indian music.

In the second half of the 17th century, *Faquir Ullah* wrote two works in *Persian* including *Rag Darpan.* In 1724 the *Sangitaparijata* was translated into *Persian* by *Pandit Dinanath.* These translations were essential as the *Hindu* mythological and religious subjects were in *Sanskrit.*

In the second half of the 18th century at the time when British assertion in the Indian political scenario became increasingly prominent, musicians dispersed to the various courts and palaces of noblemen throughout the country. Significantly, it was around this time that a treatise entitled "*On the Musical Modes of the Hindus*" was written in 1799 by *Sir William Jones,* the renowned Oriental scholar.

The Hindi *Sangit Sar* (c. 1800 A.D.) was compiled on the conclusion of the conference of leading musicians that took place in the Court of the *Maharaja* of *Jaipur, Sawai Pratap Singh.* The *Naghmat-i-Asafi* (1813 A.D.) written in Persian by

Plate 7. Miya Tansen, Famous Musician of Akbar's Court, Mughal.

Plate 8. Raga Bhairava, Kangra, Pahari.

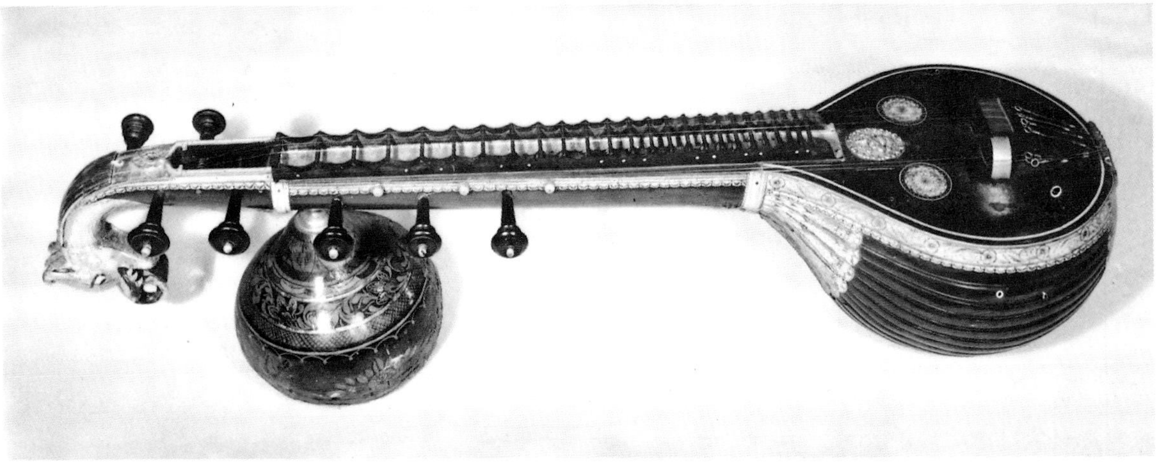

Plate VII. Veena, Tanjore.

Muhammad Reza, a nobleman of *Patna,* is reputed to be the first reliable authority in which *Bilawal Thata* is referred to as the *Shuddha* (Natural) scale. From all accounts, it appears that until about the 19th century, the Natural Scale described in North Indian texts was based on *Sadjagrama* comparable to the D mode (the ecclesiastic Dorian—the mode represented by the white keys of the piano, beginning on D). Today the *Bilawal Thata* comparable to the Western Major Scale or the C mode (the ecclesiastic Ionian) is generally accepted as the Natural Scale.

A Treatise on the Music of Hindusthan, written by *Captain N. Augustus Willard* in 1834, drew attention to the gap between musical theory and practice. *K. Banarji,* in *Gita Sutra Sara* (1855), made a sincere attempt to bridge the gap and integrate the two.

In 1914 *Fox Strangways* wrote *Music of Hindostan,* a commendable attempt to relate the numerous aspects of Indian music. His comments on contemporary Indian music are extremely enlightening. Particularly so are his analogies with Western music. The book is also a scholarly treatise and is indeed unique having been based on first-hand sources and on considerable field work undertaken by the author. Whether it be an analysis of the basic features, principles and systems or *Hindustani* music or a fascinating discussion on Indian folk music, lullabies, bardic songs and devotional songs, the work is one of sustained interest.

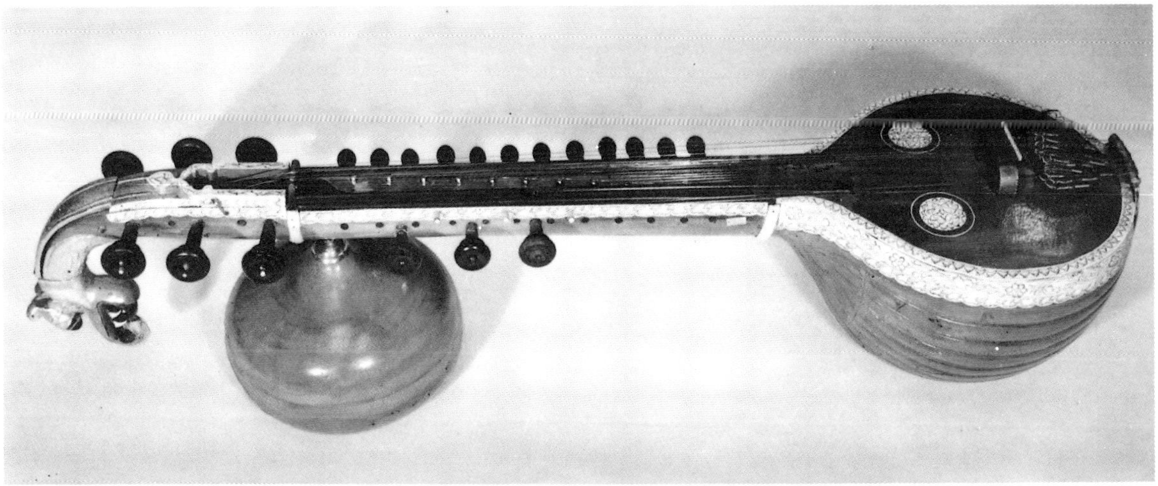

Plate VIII. Gottuvadyam, Tamil Nadu.

The works of *Pandit Vishnu Narayan Bhatkande* dominate the beginning of the 20th century. His main intention was the reconciliation of musical theory with practice. His first important work was *Srimallaksyasangitam*, followed by *Hindusthani Sangit Paddhati* and *Karamik Pustak Malika,* in six volumes. Devoted to the notation of more than 2,000 traditional songs in different *Ragas* and *Talas* collected from various *Gharanas* (family traditions), the book contains quotations from various *Sanskrit* and *Hindi* sources. *Bhatkande* has interpreted at length the musical characteristics of these *Ragas.*

Another notable work was the *Sangit-Sara-Samgraha* written in 1932 by one of the greatest patrons of Indian art: *Raja Sir Sourindra Mohun Tagore.* The work offers an in-depth study of the old *Sanskrit* texts.

A work of great analytical value is *H.L. Roy's "Problems of Hindustani Music"* (Calcutta, 1937) wherein he has highlighted the inadequacies of the present day terminology and offered suggestions for the reconstruction of musical theory. *G.H. Ranade's* work, *"Hindustani Music: An Outline of its Physics and Aesthetics"*, is particularly valuable for its analysis of the acoustics of the drone.

The present attempt to summarise the development of music would be seriously wanting and imperfect without a reference to the highly innovative contribution of *Gurudev Rabindranath Tagore,* whose experiments on harmonious compositions are not only technically but also aesthetically of a very high order. The compositions included *Dhrupad, Thumri* and *Tappa.* He also drew extensively from *Bengali* folk tunes such as *Sari, Baul* and *Keertan.*

Plate 9. Ragini Devagandhari, Kangra.

Plate 10. Raga Hindola, Malwa, Central India.

While concluding this chapter, it is considered advisable to emphasise the fact that historical perspective can only, at best, provide a backdrop against which contemporary art can be better appreciated. It is true that the process of cultural evolution has given us two systems of music: the *Hindustani* and the *Karnatak*, whether the two are the result of bifurcation of a more ancient single system of Indian music or are the consequence of fusion of regional styles has and will continue to be a subject matter of deliberation. However, what is important is that both systems are Indian, sharing a high degree of commonness while at the same time being quite clearly distinctive.

Thus a study of the evolution of Indian classical music over the centuries reveals that certain fundamental changes have taken place in the aspects relating to composition, presentation, style and content. However, due to the inner dynamism and resilience of the character of Indian music, the basic essentials and nature after assimilation and synthesis remain the same.

CHAPTER II

Evolution of the Contemporary Systems of Hindustani and Karnatak Classical Music—The Spirit of Synthesis

"There is one height of truth
and there are those who
approach from all sides, as
many sides as there are
radii in a circle, that is to
say, by routes of an infinite
variety. Let us work, then, with all
our strength to arrive at this light of
Truth which unites us all."

—*Tolstoy*

Over the centuries, two distinct systems of music have evolved in India—the *Hindustani* system of the North and the *Karnatak* of the South. In the 13th century, *Sangitaratnakara* was written in the Deccan, just on the eve of the Muslim conquest of the region by *Ala-ud-Din Khalji*. It is shortly after this that one notices a gradual differentiation between the two musical systems and styles, although they drew from one common fountainhead and heritage.

Around the 14th century, waves of foreign cultures swept across Northern India and eventually Muslim rulers established their political supremacy and control. The view expressed by *Amir Khusrau*, who commented that the music of India was one of the finest in the world, is fairly representative of the popular attitude towards Indian music prevailing at that time. Although musicians from *Iran, Afghanistan* and *Kashmir* were at the Court of the *Mughal Emperors Akbar, Jahangir* and *Shah Jahan* in the 16th and 17th centuries, it is evident that it was Indian music which captured the imagination of the Muslim rulers.

Famous Indian musicians such as *Swami Haridas, Tansen* and *Baiju Bavra* have left their indelible mark on the historical canvas of *Hindustani* music, not only as innovators and composers but also as performers. Muslim musicians further enriched the traditions of Indian music by inventing new *ragas, talas*, musical styles and forms as also by increasing the repertoire of musical instruments. This pronounced influence was also one of the contributing factors that was instrumental in accentuating the differentiation in the two styles.

Further, two main effects of royal patronage on the music of North India were clearly discernible. The first was the de-emphasis of the importance of the words in classical songs, originally composed in *Sanskrit* and which by and large were practically incomprehensible to anyone less than a traditional scholar. Hence it came to be that *Sanskrit* songs were gradually replaced by compositions in various popular dialects such as *Bhojpuri* and *Dakhani* in addition to some compositions in *Persian* and *Urdu*. However, despite this trend, Muslim musicians sometimes rendered songs with Hindu religious themes, while Hindu musicians often sang songs dedicated to Muslim saints. Perhaps the finest example of this broadminded attitude is apparent in the poetry of the *Sultan Ibrahim Adil Shah II of the Deccan*, who in his *Kitab-i-Nauras*, composed at the beginning of the 17th century, composed poems in praise of both Hindu deities and Muslim saints. The second effect of extension of royal patronage was the generation of an atmosphere of a healthy competition amongst musicians. While rendering traditional themes, considerable importance was assigned to the skill displayed by the performer in terms of imagination, interpretation and improvisation.

The period also witnessed the movement of many scholars and musicians towards the Southern part of India. These included a number of devoutly orthodox musicians who felt that their art and language should be safeguarded and cultivated. Thus we find that in the South, several musicians were in the service of Hindu rulers, and in many instances the temples also function as "patrons" for performing artistes. Every temple had a large courtyard where concerts and discussions could be held and in this manner there was considerable interaction and interface on the part of the common people with classical music, as anyone who was interested could attend musical performances rendered at the temples.

In the North, on the other hand, classical music continued largely to be restricted to the royal courts and to small groups of wealthy men who could afford to keep musicians in their household.

In the light of the above, it is not difficult to understand as to why and how language came to play a significant role in the evolution of the two systems. *Sanskrit* which was originally the first language of *Hindustani* music, was gradually replaced by *Brij Bhasha* language. While in the South, apart from *Sanskrit*, the principal languages were *Telugu, Tamil* and *Kannada*.

In general, *Karnatak* music is characterised and structured by a great degree of precision and rigidity in framework and is based on a strictly organised system. The percentage of fixed compositions rendered by artistes is also relatively

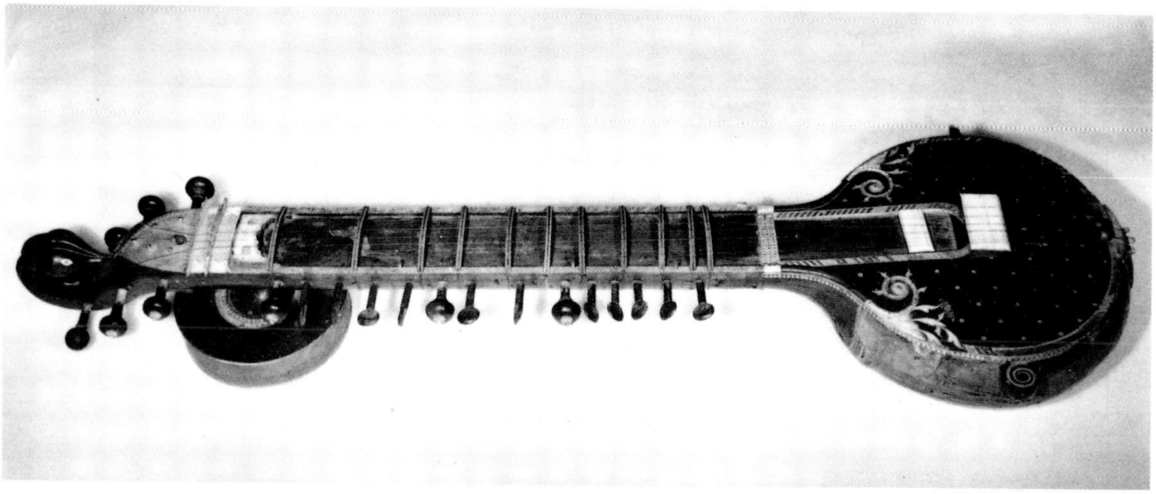

Plate IX. Sur Bahar,
Rajasthan.

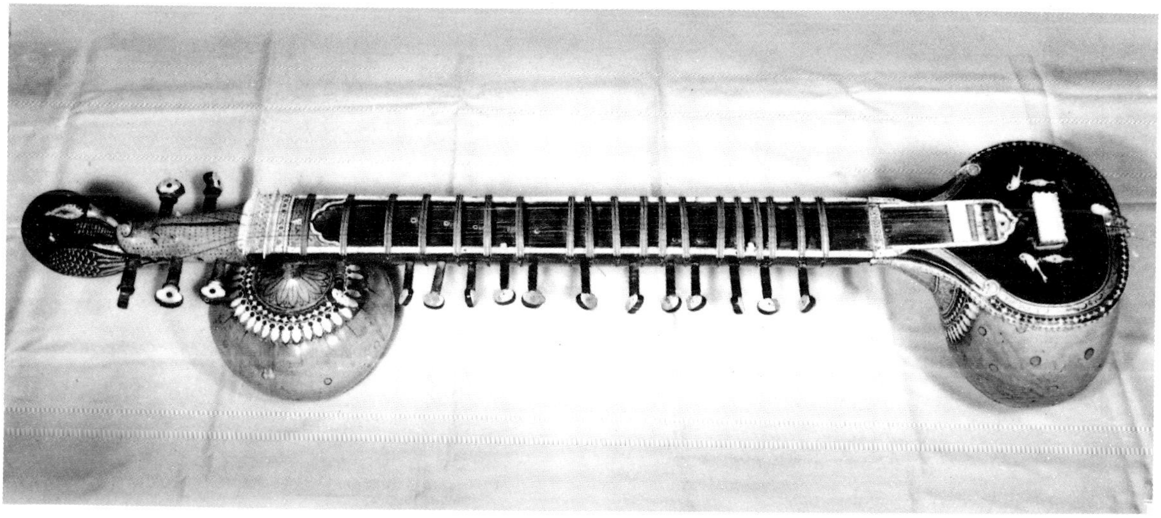

Plate X. Sitar,
Rajasthan.

Plate XII. Sur Singar,
Bengal.

high in *Karnatak* music. In fact one of the primary differences between *Karnatak* and *Hindustani* music is that while embellishments on fixed compositions is one of the prime elements of a *Karnatak* musical performance, in the *Hindustani* system, greater emphasis is placed upon improvisation. Further, in the *Karnatak* system, instrumental music very closely follows the vocal pattern.

However, despite the variegated approach and presentation, the common heritage is apparent. Some of the *Hindustani Ragas* that were played in the South were given altered names. For example, the *Hindustani Jhinjoti* was renamed *Serinjoti* in *Karnatak* music and the *Raga Kafi* became *Raga Kapi*. Then there are some *ragas*

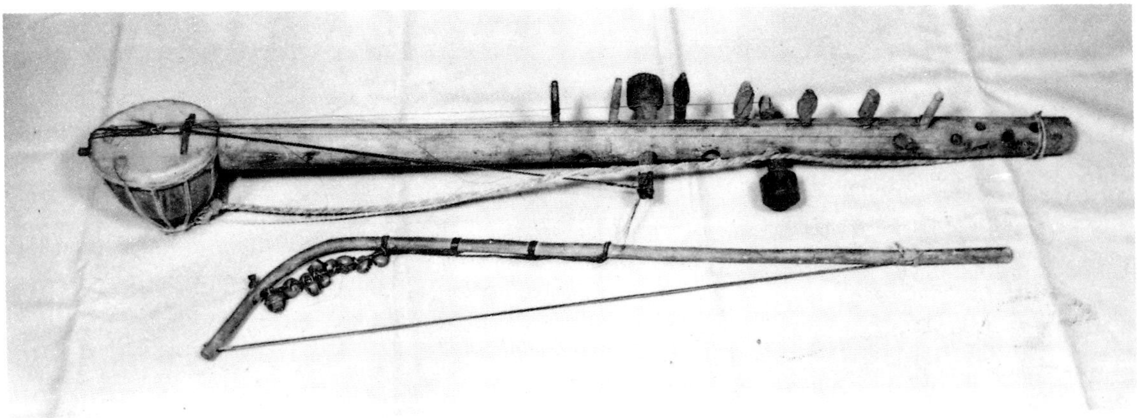

Plate XIII. Ravanahatha, Rajasthan.

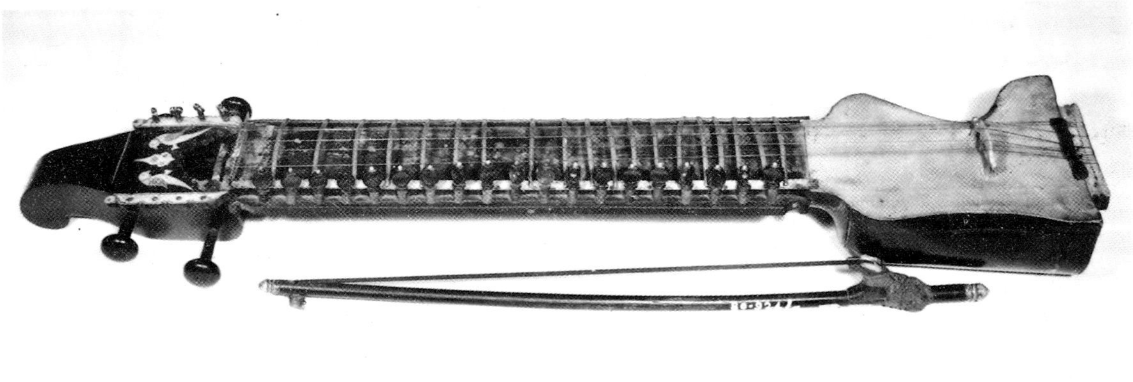

Plate XIV. Dilruba, Uttar Pradesh.

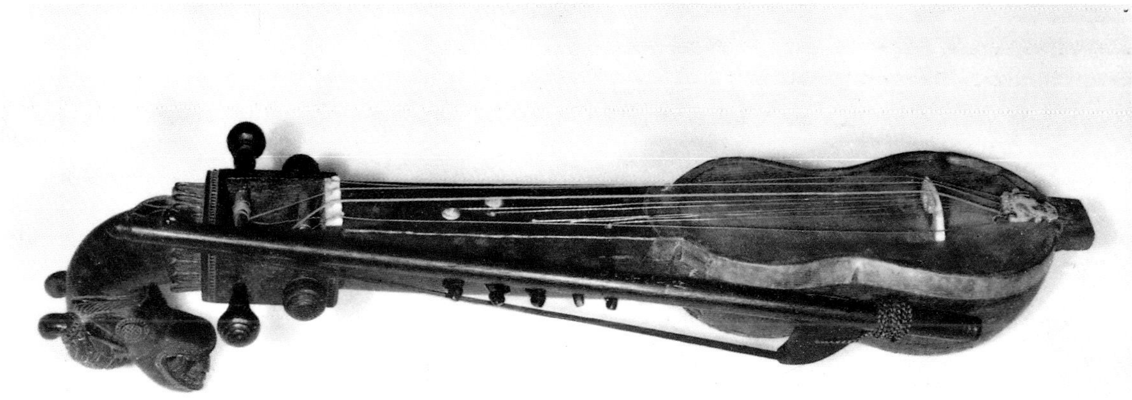

Plate XV. Sarangi, Hyderabad, Andhra Pradesh.

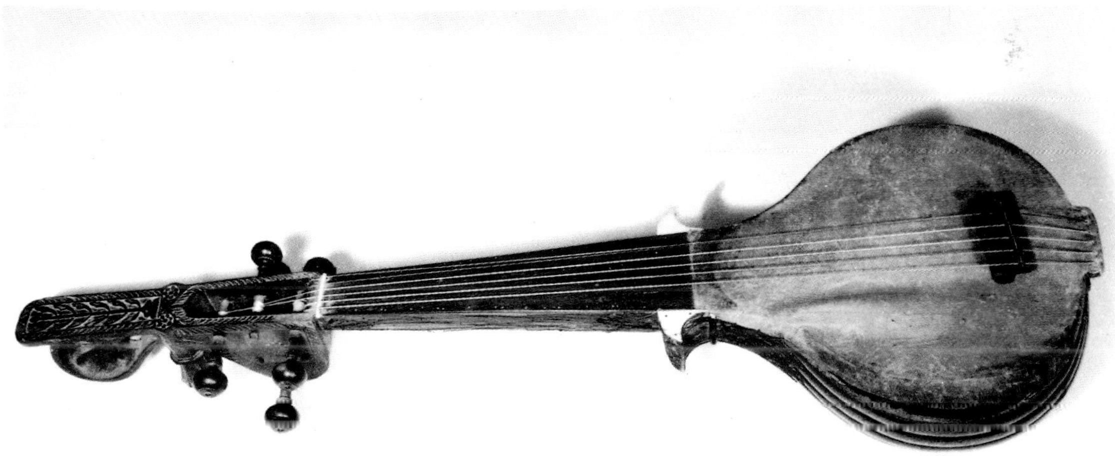

Plate XVI. Personal Rabab of Shri Jodha Bhatt, Bengal.

that have approximately the same notes in both systems but have entirely different names. *Raga Malkauns* of the North corresponds to *Raga Hindolam* of the South, the *Hindustani Raga Bhupali* is the *Raga Mohanam* while *Raga Durga* is *Raga Suddhasaveri*. Some typical *Hindustani ragas* such as *Bihag, Khamaj* and *Sindhi Bhairavi* more or less retained their original names in *Karnatak* music. Interestingly, in many cases, a typical *Karnatak raga* may have the same name as a *Hindustani* one and yet be quite different. The *Karnatak Todi, Bhairavi, Kannada* and *Sahana* are among a few in both the systems of music, where the octave is composed of twelve basic semitones. In *Karnatak* music, a great deal of emphasis is also placed on *Sampurna* (heptatonic) scale types, *Melas*, as a means of classifying *ragas*. As stated in the previous chapter, the 17th century text *Chaturdandiprakasika* lists out all the possible *melas* which could fit into the *Karnatak* system of music. This 72 *Melakarata* system still provides the basis of classification in *Karnatak* music.

The chart given below enlists the contemporary *Karnatak* notes along with their *Hindustani* equivalents, with their comparable Western notes and scales.

Hindustani	Karnatak	Solfa	Scale of C	Tone	Ratio	*Sruti*	Symbol
Shadja	*Shadjam*	Doh	C				*Sa*
Komal rishabh	*Suddha rishabham*		C#,D*b*	Major	$^{9}/_{8}$	4	*ri*
Suddha rishabh	*Chatussruti rishabham* (*Suddha gandharam*)	Re	D				*Ri*
Komal gandhar	*Sadharana gandharam* (*Shatsruti rishabham*)		D#E*b*	Minor	$^{10}/_{9}$	3	*ga*
Suddha gandhar	*Antara gandharam*	Mi	E				*Ga*
Suddha madh-yam	*Suddha madhyamam*	Fa	F	Semi	$^{16}/_{15}$	2	*Ma*
Teevra madhyam	*Prati madhyamam*		F#	Maj	$_{9}/^{8}$	4	*ma*
Pancham	*Panchamam*	Sol	G				*Pa*
Komal dhaivat	*Suddha dhaivatam*		G#,A*b*	Maj	$_{9}/^{8}$	4	*dha*
Suddha dhaivat	*Chatussruti dhaivatam* (*Suddha mishadam*)	La	A				*Dha*
Komal nishad	*Kaisiki nishadam* *Shatsruti dhaivatam*		A#,B*b*	Min	$^{10}/_{9}$	3	*ni*
Suddha nishad	*Kakali nishadam*	Ti	B	Semi	$^{16}/_{15}$	2	*Ni*
(*Tara shadja*)	(*Tara shadjam*)	Doh	C^1				Sa^1

Note: If all the *srutis* are added from *Sa* to Sa^1 they will total up to 22. And if all the ratios are multiplied by one another they will give a product of 2. This is the measure of an octave or a *sthayi.*

CHAPTER III

Romance of the Raga

"There should be rhythm,
there should be melody,
but there should be peace.
There should be metre and prosody,
there should be no confusion,....
but there should be the love of the Lord in the song."

—Purandara dasa

The word *"Sangeet"* has a complex connotation. It signifies the union of three elements—*gita, vadya* and *nritya*; or song, percussion and dance.

The principles and laws governing both vocal and instrumental music, as also the rules and directions with regard to the entire scope of theatric representation, are collectively termed as *Sangeet Shastra.*

Sangeet Shastra could be regarded both as a science and as an art. Viewed as a science, it deals with the origin of *Nada* or sound; of the doctrines of *Sruti, swara,* scale and the grammatical structure of the *Raga.* Considered as an art, it lays down the necessary directions for the cultivation of the human voice; norms for the performance of instrumental music; and the essence of the various gestures and motions in dance. It is divided into two categories: viz. *aupapattika* and *krisidha,* or theory and practice.

According to Indian tradition, sound is God—*Nada Brahma. Nada* or intelligible sound results from the union of physical breath with the fire of intellect. In other words musical sound and musical experience are steps in the path of self-realisation. Thus music is viewed as a spiritual discipline that elevates one's inner self to the attainment of divine peacefulness and goals. The *Ragas* are among the means through which God can be reached. They form the heart and core of our music. Thus the most essential characteristic of *Gita, Vadya* and *Nritya* is *Rakti* or the power of reaching out to the heart.

The Author at a Sitar Performance 1974.

According to the ancient scriptures, there are two types of sound. The *Sangitamakaranda* distinguishes between the two kinds. The first kind is *Anahata nada* or "unstruck sound", which is caused by the vibration of ether, the upper or purer air near heaven. It is regarded as the sound of the universe—ever present and unchanging! The other kind of sound is called the *Ahata nada* or "struck sound" because it is caused by physical impact. For the *Yogis* the *Anahata nada* is most significant as it is the eternal sound they seek from within and which can be heard only after long years of meditation and discipline in *Yoga.* Through *Tapasya,* the *Yogi* tries to awaken the *Kundalini,* the divine creative force within man, which resides in the central part of the body at the root of the spine. According to the doctrine of *Yoga,* at an advanced stage of self-realisation and spiritual development, this power is awakened and moves up the spine to the other *Chakras* to open up the "Thousand-Petalled" lotus in the brain which is said to give the *Yogi* complete physical and spiritual control.

Coming to manifested musical sounds through the *Raga*, the heart and soul of Indian classical music, there is a saying in *Sanskrit—"Ranjayati iti Ragah"*— which means "*That which colours the mind is a raga*". The *Raga* is the colour which is lent to the blank canvas of the receptive human mind. It would be befitting to explain at this stage the concepts of *Sruti* and *Swara*. *Sruti* forms the basis on which the superstructure of the *Raga* is built. In the musical sense, *Sruti* is a particle of sound, perceivable by the ear. It is an essential element in the formation of tones of which a *Saptaka* or Octave is composed. Each *Saptaka* is divided into twenty-two *Srutis*. A *Swara* or note or musical sound is the aggregate of a number of *Srutis*. The *Swaras* or notes are the same in number as in the West. Every note or *Swara* in the *Raga* carries with it a certain expression or emotion. The total expression of notes forming part of a *Raga* creates an intensely powerful musical entity or form.

Plate XVII. Santoor, Kashmir.

The above concepts of *Swara* and *Sruti* and their interrelationship have been described in a lucid manner by *Sarangadeva* and *Visvabasu.*

Referring to the character and qualities of the *Swara* that is derived from the *Sruti, Sarangadeva* states thus:

Jah snigdho anurananatmaka
Svato ranjayati srotricittang sa svara ucyaytey

(What is soft, what is of the form of resonance, what gives aesthetic joy to the mind of the hearer, that is called a svara.)

Visvabasu, an ancient musicologist, refers to *Sruti* as that sound which is discernible to the listener:

sravanendriyagrajhyatvad dhvanireva srutirbhavet

From the above it can be deduced that *Sruti* is responsible for the origin of *Swara.*

The *Raga,* which is indeed the superstructure and the edifice, may be defined as a musical form of *Swaras* having a permitted manner of ascent or *Aroha* (*Arohana*) and a permitted manner of descent or *Avaroha* (*Avarohana*). *Ragas* may be *Audav* (pentatonic), *Shadava* (hexatonic) or *Sampurna* (heptatonic). The number of possible *Ragas* is indeed infinite. Scholars have concluded that given the total number of 72 parent scales, with all their permutations and combinations, each scale could give rise to hundreds of different possible patterns, thus making the number of possible *Ragas* boundless and unlimited! Therefore, it can never be said that a musician "invents" a *Raga.* He could at best "discover" one.

Apart from *Aroha* and *Avaroha,* there are certain recognizable phrases and features of a *Raga* that serve to identify it and give it a distinctive flavour and character. Referred to as *Svaroop, Pakad* or *Chalan* meaning "motion" or "movement" this is a more detailed and subtle concept which introduces to the *Raga* the main features of distinction, grace and rhythm. *Shadja or Sa* (tonic) is the base note in a *Raga* apart from which each *Raga* has a predominant note known as the "*Vadi*" (sonant). It is this which infuses a particular sentiment, mood or emotion into the entire *Raga.* The *Samvadi* is the note which is generally at the interval of a fourth or fifth from the *Vadi* and serves to strengthen the expression of the *Vadi* (sonant). The other notes in the scale of a *Raga* are termed as *Anuvadi* (assonants). All other notes outside a given scale are termed *"Vivadi"* (enemies).

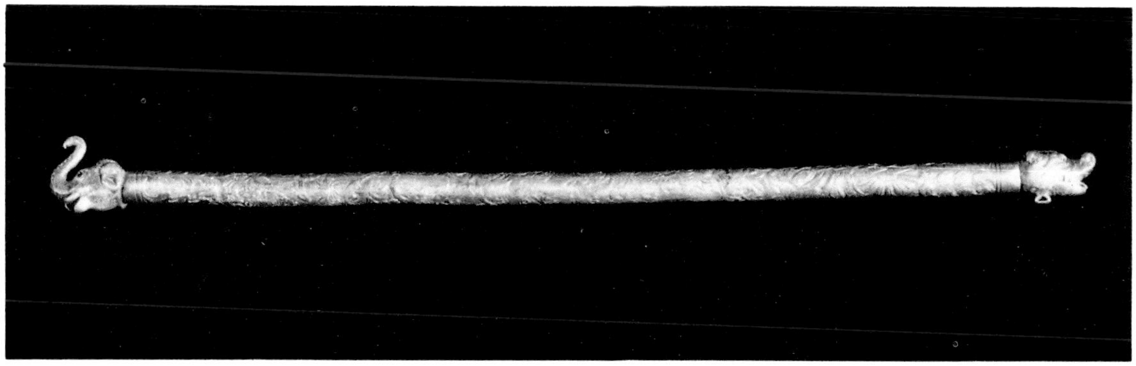

Plate XVIII. Flute (silver, side-playing), North India.

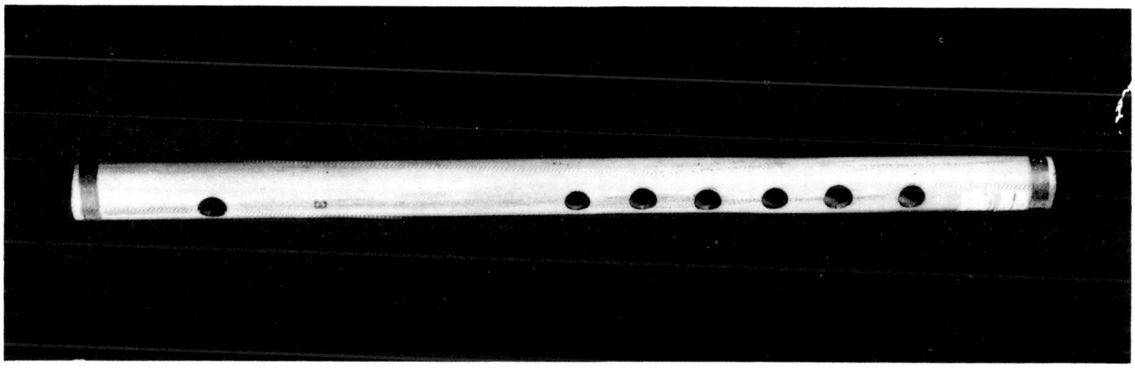

Plate XIX. Flute (bamboo, side-playing), Assam.

The texture of the *Raga* is created through various devices and embellishments which test and prove the finesse, skill, creativity and aesthetic sensibilities of the performing artiste. The *Gamakas* or grace notes, the *Kampita* (a shake), the *Andolita* (sounding more than one note with one stroke) and *Tiripa* (stressing one note of a phrase) are all methods used for the ornamentation and refinement of a *Raga* so as to crystallize its true mood, meaning and structure and evoke the intended sentiments and emotions.

It would be pertinent to elucidate herein the concept of *Nava Rasa* or the "nine sentiments". Literally, "*Rasa*" means juice but in terms of art, it would mean "emotion" or "sentiment". The performing arts in India whether they be music, dance, drama or even poetry, are based on the concept of *Nava Rasa.* Each *Raga* or even each artistic creation is supposed to be dominated by at least one of these nine sentiments. The closer the association of a *Raga* with a sentiment, the more pronounced would be its effect.

Plate 12 (on page 51). Raga Megha, Kangra, Pahari.

Plate 11. Raga Hindola and Ragini Telangi, Deccan or Gwalior.

The first *Rasa* is *Shringara,* a romantic sentiment. *Hasya* is the second and is intended to be comic and to provoke laughter. The third is *Karuna* reflecting pathos, loneliness and longing for either God or lover. Fury or anger is reflected in *Raudra,* while *Veera* expresses bravery and heroism. *Bhayanaka* is the sixth *Rasa* which denotes fear and fright, while *Vibhatsa* portrays disgust. The eighth *Rasa* is *Adbhuta* showing wonderment, amazement and exhilaration. The last *Rasa* is *Shanta*—reflecting peace, tranquillity and contentment.

Thus, from the above analysis of the concept of a *Raga* it can be surmised that a *Raga* is in reality an aesthetic projection and portrayal, as also a spiritual transformation of a designed and structured grammatical musical base.

CHAPTER IV

Tala—The Rhythm of Life

"You can work it out by Fractions
or by the simple Rule of Three
But the way of Tweedledum
is not the way of Tweedledee."

—The Jungle Book

Apart from *Raga,* the second fundamental element of Indian classical music is *Tala.* The word *Tala* according to tradition has derived its origin from the syllables *Ta* (from *Tandava,* the cosmic dance of *Lord Shiva*) and *La* (from *Lasya,* the feminine counterpart of *Tandava*; a dance originally attributed to *Goddess Parvati,* the consort of *Lord Shiva*). Another interpretation of the word *Tala* is that it refers to hand clapping for keeping time. *Tala* in its micro sense denotes an organised rhythmic cyclical pattern composed of various *Matras* or units.

The complexity of *Tala* in Indian music is apparent from the fact that one rhythmic cycle could vary from 3 to 108 beats, or more although there are generally about 15 to 20 *Talas* most often adopted by musicians. Another 40 *Talas* are sometimes performed for an audience possessing a deep and specialised understanding of the music.

Just as the notes employed in a *Raga* vary in importance, so also the beats in each *Tala* have different degrees of importance. The most strongly emphasised beat is the *Sam* (*Sama*) which is the most emphatic of all moments as it commences the cycle and is a kind of centre of gravity in a circle. After having negotiated various cycles of improvisation, the *Sam* is the focal point at which the artiste arrives: a point that the listeners are eagerly waiting for!

The second crucial point in the rhythmic cycle is called *Khali* (the unstressed or empty beat). It is shown by the wave of the hand, without giving an audible beat. In *Karnatak* music, it is termed as *Veesu* or *Visarjitam.*

TALA IN HINDUSTANI MUSIC

In *Hindustani* music, there are three main tempos or rhythmical patterns. They are *Vilambit* (slow), *Madhyam* (moderate) and *Drut* (fast). There is also the *Ati Drut* (very fast). Among the more frequently used *Talas* are:

Dadra Six beats, grouped 3+3. This is primarily used for the light classical style known as *Dadra*. It is also popular for folk music, *Bhajans*, *Qawali*, *Ghazals* and other forms of light classical music.

Rupak Seven beats, grouped 3+2+2, generally played on *Tabla* as accompaniment to either vocal or instrumental music in the *Khyal* style.

Teental Sixteen beats, grouped 4+4+4+4. This is the most popular *Tala* used by vocalists as well as instrumentalists performing in any tempo.

Jhaptal Ten beats grouped 2+3+2+3. This can be used to accompany *Khyal* music. It is also played on the *Pakhawaj* to accompany a *Sadra* composition, a medium-fast *Dhrupad* song.

The Author Performing on the Sitar, accompanied by Shri Dilshad Ahmad Khan on the Tabla. Venue: Hyderabad.

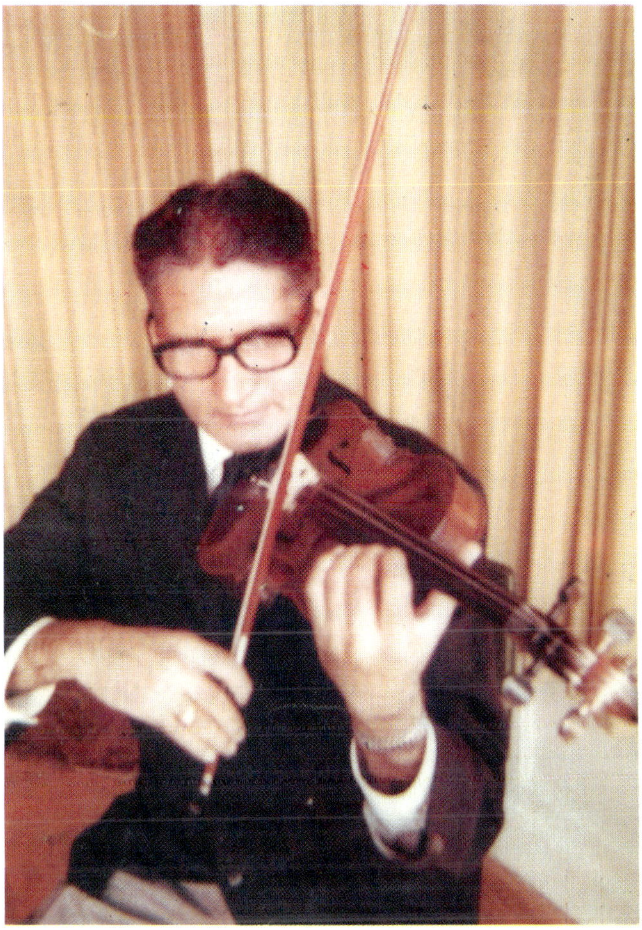

Guru Shri S.N. Gulati playing the Violin.

Kaharwa Eight beats, grouped 4+4. This is used for light classical and popular music as in *Dadra Tala*.

Ektal Twelve beats, grouped as 4+4+2+2. This is played on the *Tabla* exclusively for *Khyal* compositions.

Chautal Twelve beats, grouped as 4+4+2+2. This is used mostly in *Dhrupad* compositions and was widely played on a variety of the older generation instruments.

Dhamar Fourteen beats, grouped as 5+5+4. This is played on the *Pakhawaj* often to accompany the traditional songs for the *Holi* Festival of spring.

Jhumra Fourteen beats, grouped as 3+4+3+4. This is generally used in accompaniment for *Khyal* compositions in very slow tempo and is rendered on *Tabla*.

Charchar Fourteen beats, grouped as 3+4+3+4. This *Tala* is played mostly on the *Tabla* as accompaniment to light *Thumri* compositions, although it may also be used to accompany string and wind instruments.

The accompaniment of the *Tabla* is known as *Sangat.* In *Jawabi Sangat* the *Tabla* player in any tempo imitates a phrase executed by the instrumentalist. In *Sath* (together) *Sangat,* the *Tabla* tries to closely follow the rhythmic patterns executed by the instrumentalist and the most exhilarating moment is reached when both simultaneously playing the same phrases meet on the *Sam.* In *Larant* (fighting) *Sangat,* the dialogues are even more exciting. There is also *Sawaal Jawab* (question and answer) between the instrumentalist and percussionist. Another challenging form of rendering is the *Jugalbandi* which could be a dialogue between two or more instrumentalists, wherein the skill of the artist is determined not only by his interpretation of the *Raga* that is being rendered but also by his ability to harmonise and synthesise with his co-performers the intricacies of the *Tala* as also the *Rasas* or sentiments and emotions that distinguish the *Raga,* that he performs.

TALA IN KARNATAK MUSIC

Tala in *Karnatak* music has been fitted into a scheme of temporal divisions. This scheme is rigorously followed. The basic aspect of the scheme is the quantification of time, the smallest interval of which is the *Kshana (*an instant). This is measured as the time taken "*to pierce with a pin the hundred lotus leaves placed one above another*". As many as 16,384 *Kshanas* constitute one *Anudruta* or *Akshara,* the practical unit of musical time and the brick out of which all further sections are constructed. An *Anudruta* is obtained as follows:

8 *Kshanas* = 1 *Lava*

8 *Lavas* = 1 *Kashta*

8 *Kashtas* = 1 *Nimisha*

8 *Nimishas* = 1 *Kala*

2 *Kalas* = 1 *Chaturbhaga*

2 *Chaturbhagas* = 1 *Anudruta*

The further combinations of common usage are the *Druta* (*2 Aksharas*), *Laghu* (*4 Aksharas*) and *Guru* (*8 Aksharas*). The *Akshara* does not have a specific or objective time measure. In other words, it cannot be measured in terms of a watch or a metronome, although a certain traditional habit has given it an accepted time length. Depending therefore on its duration, the *Akshara* can have three degrees of tempo or *Laya.* These are the *Vilamba Laya* (slow), *Madhyama Laya* (medium) and *Druta Laya* (fast). Each *Laya* is twice as fast as the preceding one. The *Madhyama Laya* is double the speed of *Vilamba* while *Druta* is double that of *Madhyama.* In the parlance of a *Karnatak* musician, *Laya* is often referred to as *Kala*; *Vilamba Laya* is thus *Chowka Kala.*

A *Tala* is constructed out of a choice of three limbs or sections, known as *Angas,* which vary on account of their difference in duration. The three *Angas* are *Anudruta, Druta* and *Laghu.* While the first consists of one *Akshara* and the *Druta* of two, the *Laghu* is of a variable duration of 3, 4, 5, 7 or 9 *Aksharas. Anudruta* is counted by a beat; *Druta* by a beat and a wave of the hand; *Laghu* by a beat and count of fingers: say a *Laghu* of 5 units by a beat plus counting of four fingers.

Some of the *Talas* popularly performed in the concerts of *Karnatak* music are as follows:

Adi Tala Grouped as 4+2+2
(*Chaturasra Jati Triputa*)

Roopaka Tala Grouped as 2+4
(*Chaturasra Jati Roopaka*)

Jhampa Tala Grouped as 7+1+2
(*Misra Jati Jhampa*)

Chapu Tala Grouped as 3+4
(*Misra Chapu*)

Khanda Chapu Tala Grouped as 2+3

In actual practice, *Roopaka* is not set as 2+4 but often as 2+2+2. Interestingly, the *Chapu Tala* is believed to have been derived from folk music.

It is thus apparent that the fundamental concepts and basis of construction of *Tala,* in both the *Hindustani* and *Karnatak* systems, are broadly based upon similar parameters. In both, *Tala* is thus conceived as a cyclic measure. Interestingly, in both the systems, there are also *Talas* which possess very complex combinations. However despite the degree of complexity apart, among the popularly used rhythmic patterns or *Talas* in the *Hindustani* system, is the *Teental,* comprising 16 beats, grouped as 4+4+4+4 and the *Aditala* in the *Karnatak* system, grouped as 8 beats, in an arrangement of 4+2+2.

However, despite the similarities, certain subtle distinctions between the two systems are worth elaboration.

The first difference is explained herewith. As in the *Karnatak* system, the fundamental unit of time in *Hindustani* music is the *Matra* which is equivalent to the *Anudruta* or *Akshara* of *Karnatak* music. Here again the *Matra* is of an arbitrary and subjective time value. It may be long, medium or short in duration. When long, it gives a slow *Vilambit,* when medium, a *Madhya* and when short a fast or *Druta* tempo.

In actual practice, however, there is one essential difference between the two systems. In *Karnatak* music, the proportion of three *Layas* is maintained, i.e. the *Madhyama* is strictly twice the speed of the *Vilamba* and the *Druta* twice of *Madhyama.* As the musicians there say, there is an adherence to *Kala Pramana* (temporal ratio). However in the *Hindustani* system, particularly in the current style in which *Khyal* is rendered as also in instrumental music, there is no such rigidity. The tempo is thus increased gradually from very slow to very fast. A rhythmic composition is usually started in *Vilambit Laya* and the tempo is accelerated, without a specifically measured pace. Sometimes separate compositions are performed for slow and fast music. However, it is significant to note that in the *Dhrupad* style of singing, a uniformity of tempo is maintained throughout.

The second distinction is as follows. The section of *Tala,* which is the *Anga,* is commonly referred to as a *Khand* in *Hindustani* music. Of these the common ones are *Anudruta* (one *Matra*), the *Druta* (two *Matras*). The use of the concept of *Laghu,* as in *Karnatak* music is however not there. A *Laghu* in the *Hindustani* system is of 4 *Matras,* the other types not being employed. The larger sections of the *Tala* can be of 3, 4, 5 or more *Matras.* What is of greater importance is that in the *Hindustani* system, a *Tala* can have heterogeneous *Laghus,* a fact not met with in *Karnatak* music.

Thus it can be said that the study of the structure and grammar of rhythm in Indian classical music is a fascinating one indeed. It has the distinction of having attained a high degree of sophistication. The distribution and division of the time involved in the art of percussion, while simultaneously relating the same to the musical composition, the gradual acceleration of tempo along with subtle cross rhythms and syncopation, is indeed an art requiring proficiency and skill, concentration, imagination and *Sadhana.*

CHAPTER V

Raga Presentation—A Wealth of Styles

To fill the temple court with joy,
To chase the city's gloom away;
The heart to still, the passions calm,
Of weeping eyes the tears to stay.

—*From an Inscription of Gudea,*
Sumerian Priest-King, c. 2400 B.C.

Indian classical music is generally based on two movements. While the first is in free time and not accompanied by percussion, the second is in a fixed time-measure invariably accompanied by drums. The first movement constitutes the *Alap* or *Alapana* with which most Indian classical music begins. It is slow, serene, spiritual, reverential and evocative—almost like an invocation or prayer. From the melodic point of view this constitutes the most important part of the performance. It is in the *Alap* that the musician gradually explores and unfolds the distinguishing characteristics of the *Raga,* without being bound by a fixed time-measure, while generally portraying the *Shanta* and *Karuna Rasas.*

Within the *Alap,* there are several stages of development leading to the section known as *Jor* or *Nom Tom* in *Hindustani* music and *Tanam* in *Karnatak.* Although this section is performed without a fixed time-measure, a distinct pulse is introduced. In the *Hindustani* system, the *Jor* often culminates in a section called *Jhala* (web) where fast rhythms are produced on the drone or *Chikari* strings, eventually culminating in the crescendo and climax.

On conclusion of the *Alap* there is a short pause when the instruments are retuned before the second movement of the *Raga* commences.

Unlike in *Hindustani* classical music, there are no purely instrumental compositions in the *Karnatak* system. In the *Hindustani* system there is a form called *Gat* which originated from the plucked stringed instrument technique and another form called *Dhun,* derived basically from folk tunes—neither of which has text. However, in both systems pride of place must be given to the human voice because of its ability to express through words as also its versatility, flexibility and capacity to glide from one pitch to another. Instrumental technique is understandably influenced by the voice although the exchange is not entirely one way. A study of the various media of music has conclusively proved that certain techniques adopted by the human voice, including the *Gayaki Ang*, have unmistakably influenced instrumental music.

DHRUPAD

In *Hindustani* classical music, within the *Raga Sangeet*, the most distinctive styles are the *Dhrupad* or *"Dhruvapad"* and *Khyal*. In the 15th century *Raja Man Singh Tomar* of *Gwalior* developed the *Dhrupad* style into an organised system. In the beginning, the song texts of *Dhrupad* were majestic praises of the Gods and Goddesses. Since this music was originally considered a means for elevating the soul and spirit to the higher echelons of consciousness, the texts of the early *Dhrupad*

Rendering Alap.

Sitar Performance accompanied by Tabla and Tanpura.

compositions were essentially of a religious nature. Gradually, however, the texts of the songs changed from praises of God to elegant praises of the kings and emperors who protected the musicians and extended to them royal patronage. Some *Dhrupads* were also sung in praise of nature. These compositions are in slow tempo with little use of ornamentation. The compositional intricacies are further developed in the succeeding two sections—*Sanchari* and *Abhog*. Each section consists of one or more lines of poetry. There are definite and positive indications that the archaic *Dhrupad* form is at present undergoing a period of revival. In structure, *Dhrupad* has four sections. Of these the *Asthayi* or *Sthayi* is the basic or first part, usually focused on the lower and middle octaves. The *Antara* is the second section exploring the middle and upper octaves.

KHYAL

The major musical style that evolved after *Dhrupad* is *Khyal,* a Muslim word meaning 'thought' or 'imagination'. In contrast to *Dhrupad, Khyal* is much less word-bound, consisting only of two parts—*Sthayi* and *Antara. Khyal* compositions are highly ornamented. There are two types of *Khyal, Bara* and *Chota.* The *Bara Khyal* is sometimes sung in extremely slow tempo where each *Matra* (unit) of the time-measure might last as long as 4 or 5 seconds and one whole cycle of the *Tala,* as long as a minute. It is also not uncommon for a vocalist to ignore the words except for the short phrase called '*Mukhra*' (face) which concludes the line and leads to the first beat of the next *Tala* cycle. As there is no set conclusion to the *Bara Khyal,* the vocalist could graduate with or without a pause to the *Chota Khyal,* the tempo of which may be as many as eight times that of the *Bara Khyal,* and thereafter progress towards the climax.

Scholars maintain that *Amir Khusrau* was instrumental in popularizing the *Khyal* style and may even have given it its name. In the 15th century, the *Sharqui* rulers actively promoted this style. Further, under the rule of *Sultan Mohammad Shah* (1719-1748), *Niyamat Khan,* who was conferred the title of *Shah Sadarang* by the *Sultan,* brought *Khyal* to its highest popularity and till today it continues to be one of the predominant styles in *Hindustani* classical music.

As in *Dhrupad,* there are four major *Gharanas* or 'families' of *Khyal.* The oldest and most comprehensive in technique is the *Gwalior Gharana,* the notable characteristics being open-throated singing and straight movements. The doyens of this *Gharana* were *Natthan Khan* and *Peer Baksh.* The *Agra Gharana* is said to have been founded by *Haji Sujan Khan* and the emphasis was on *bole tan* and syncopation. In recent times, *Faiyyaz Khan* was one of the greatest vocalists of this school. A third major school is the *Jaipur-Atroli Gharana,* the style of which is characterized by medium tempo and *alankaras* or repetitive patterns. Among the popular schools is the *Patiala Gharana* developed mainly by *Abdul Wahid Khan* and *Abdul Karim Khan.*

THUMRI

Thumri, a light melodic, semi-classical form, has its basis in the romantic religious literature inspired by the *Bhakti Movement.* It acquired great prominence and grace at the court of *Nawab Wajid Ali Shah of Lucknow,* in the later half of the 19th century. A *Thumri* is generally the *piece de resistance* of *Khyal* singers or instrumentalists. Among the finest styles of *Thumri* is the *Purab* style of *Banaras* and *Lucknow.* These romantic melodies are characterised by a sense of calm, interwoven with tranquillity and intrinsic peace not without a tinge of pathos. The tonic note *Sa* may be shifted and folk and popular songs can be included in a composition.

Thumri is essentially lyrical in approach. Further, not all *ragas* are used in *Thumri* and those that are used are amenable to the soft and romantic sentiments—e.g., *Khamaj, Kafi, Bhairavi* and *Pilu.* The emphasis is on the *Shringara Rasa,* thereby creating an atmosphere of romance, not without the pangs of separation, uncertainty and longing. There are broadly two styles of *Thumri,* one being the subdued *Purab* (Eastern) variety and the other being the more mercurial style of the *Punjab.*

TAPPA

Among the other styles of vocal music is the *Tappa,* originally a *Punjabi Muslim* folk form sung by the camel-cart drivers and later developed to a classical form by *Mian Shori. Tappas* have a continuous melody and lingering appeal, characterised by a stylised presentation with much ornamentation, rhythm, fast tempo and lyrics on love. This form remained generally confined to the North and North-West.

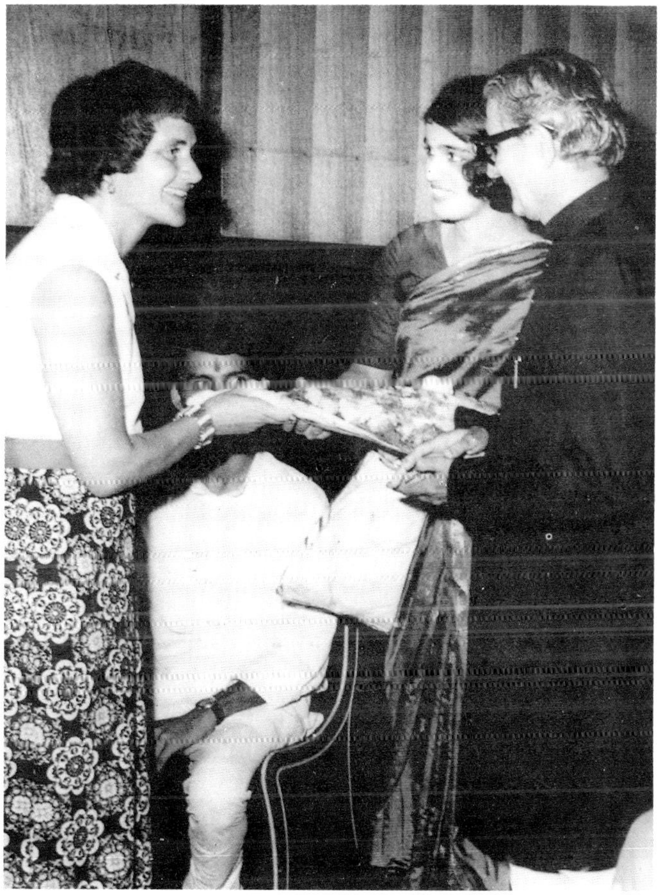

Felicitations to the Guru and the Shishya, after a Sitar Performance.

Plate 13. Raga Megha, Malwa, Central India.

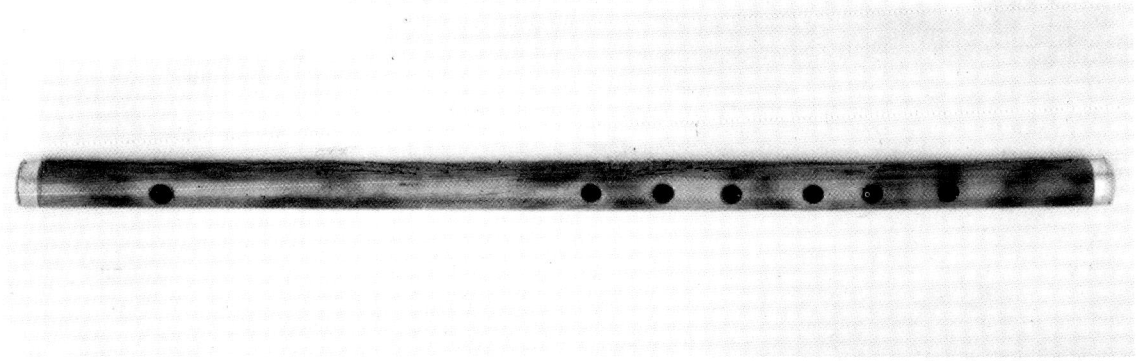

Plate XX. Flute (bamboo, side-playing), Maharashtra.

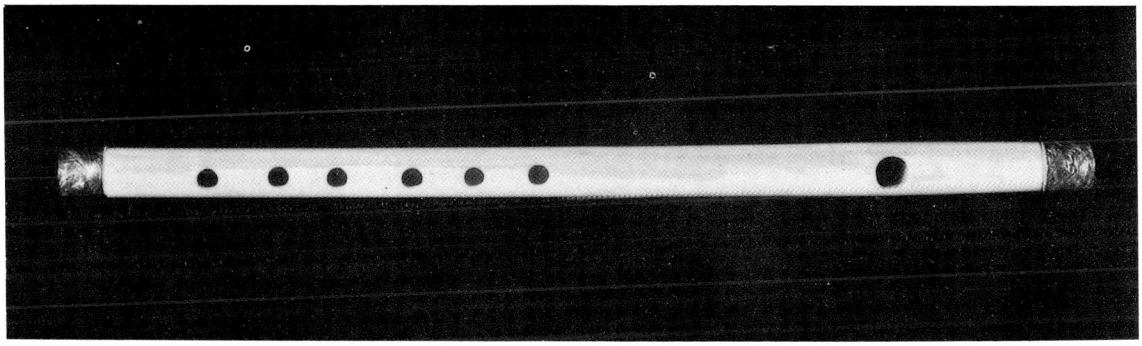

Plate XXI. Flute (side-playing, ivory with silver covered ends), Rajasthan.

TARANA

The *Tarana* is a style of singing similar to *Sargams* or *Solfeggio* exercises. Similar to the *Tillana* of *Karnatak* music, it uses as its text mnemonic syllables used for drumming or *Swara* signatures and sometimes even Persian words. *Amir Khusrau* is said to have been the innovator of this style when he was challenged in the court of *Alauddin Khalji* to reproduce in a singing contest the piece rendered by *Nayak Gopal.* Some say that the syllables used in *Taranas* are adaptations of mnemonic signatures of *Tabla* and *Sitar* strokes. While others opine that these are mutilations of *Persian* and *Arabic* words.

GHAZALS

Ghazals are another form of song derived from the *Urdu* poetic form, composed of independent couplets. The verses are open to a variety of interpretations: secular, mystical and philosophical. This form has achieved a great deal of popularity.

RAGAM-TANAM-PALLAVI

Karnatak music, as stated earlier, is characterised by an absence of purely instrumental compositions. The vocal form referred to as *Ragam-Tanam-Pallavi* is generally the main item at a *Karnatak Kacheri* (musical recital). The term *Ragam* refers to *Alapana,* unbounded by a fixed time-measure. This is followed by *Tanam,* which though rhythmic is unmeasured. The final section is the *Pallavi,* a composition of words and melody set to a particular *Tala.* The composition could either be traditional or composed by the performer himself.

The accompaniments generally include the *Violin* and *Mridangam.* Passages called *Swara Kalpana* or the Indian equivalent of *Sol-fa* syllables are substituted for parts of the original composition and the *Pallavi* is the focal point of return at the conclusion of each improvisation. It is generally customary for the *Pallavi* to be followed by a drum solo to be concluded by the brief restatement of the *Pallavi.*

The *Ragam-tanam-pallavi* is the longest item in a recital of *Karnatak* music. It reflects the skill and imagination of the performer. The *Kirtana* or *Kriti,* a devotional song, provides a blend of text, melody and rhythm. The *Kriti* may be preceded by an *Alapana* and consists of three sections called *Pallavi, Anupallavi* and *Charanam* comprising of lines of devotional poetry.

VARNAM

Other forms include the *Varnam,* a completely composed piece, designed to show a *Raga* in all its pristine purity. *Pada* and *Javali* are two kinds of love-songs depicting poetic imagery characteristic of the *Bhakti Movement.* The *Tillana* similar to the *Tarana* is rhythmic and in very fast tempo.

Thus the rich heritage of the *Raga,* in the tradition of Indian classical music, is truly a unique form of musical expression and medium, which with all its nuances and sentiments transposes both the performer and the listener to heights of Divinity and self-realisation.

CHAPTER VI

Great Composers in Karnatak Music

"As the musician knows how to tune his lyre,
so the wise man knows how to set
his mind in tune with all minds."

—Daemophilus

In view of the diversity, distinctive character and development of the two forms of Indian classical music, *Hindustani* and *Karnatak,* the contributions of the musical stalwarts of *Karnatak* music are enunciated in this chapter.

Between the 14th and 16th centuries, *Vidyaranya, Ramamatya* and *Vitthala* were among the notable scholars and musicians who helped mould the *Karnatak* system.

Purandara dasa (c. 1484-1564) a prolific composer is credited with as many as 4,75,000 songs, mostly in *Sanskrit* and *Kannada.* He succeeded in presenting the quintessence of the *Upanishads* and the *Puranas* in his compositions. Clothed in fascinatingly simple tunes, these songs are simultaneously reflective of sublime thoughts, high ideals and are characterised by beautiful similes and proverbs which make them expressive in content. His compositions are featured in *Ragas* including *Manjisa Bhairavi, Dvijavanti, Syama Kalyani, Madhumadhavi* and *Vasanta Bhairavi.* Significantly his compositions contained the signature: *Purandara Vitthala.* Realising the importance of imparting musical knowledge, he composed the *Svaravali, Alankaras, Ghanaraga Gitas* and *Prabandhas.* In fact the art form: *Kriti,* which attained unprecedented heights of perfection at the hands of *Tyagaraja,* originated with *Purandara dasa.*

Venkatamakhi, who lived in the early part of the 17th century, is well-known for his outstanding work *Caturdandi prakasika* as also for his reforms in the system of scale.

Bhadrachala Ramadas (c. 1620-1688) who is yet another revered name in the history of *Karnatak* music, is a link between the *Kirtana* composers of the earlier period and the *Kriti* composers of the later period. His songs are essentially in the *Kirtana* form with the divisions: *Pallavi, Anupallavi* and *Charana.* He had composed several *Divyanama Kirtanas* and while the majority of his works were in *Telugu,* some of them including *Narayana Narayana* and *Vande Raghurama* were rendered in *Sanskrit.* His songs are characterised by the fragrance of devotion, simplicity, depth and dignity.

The ensuing period, c. 1750-1850, was indeed a remarkable one in musical history, for during this period there flourished the three musical geniuses: *Syama Sastry, Tyagaraja* and *Muthuswami Dikshitar,* collectively referred to as the Musical Trinity or *Trimurti.*

Remarkable indeed is the coincidence that all three great men of scholarship were in fact contemporaries, proficient in *Sanskrit,* well versed in the *Vedas, Shastras,* sacred lore and belonged to *Thiruvaiyaru* in the *Tanjavur District* of South India.

Syama Sastry, born in 1762, a scholar, well versed in *Sanskrit* and *Telugu,* was an ardent devotee of Mother Goddess: *Sri Kamakshi.* He was a person who spoke to the Goddess and to whom the Goddess spoke. His mastery over *Tala* and *Laya* was indeed exceptional. He composed in intricate time-measures and signed as *Syama Krishna.* He had composed about 300 musical pieces consisting mostly of *Kritis* and a few *Svarajatis* and *Varnas.* They were in popularly known *Ragas* including *Todi, Dhanyasi, Bhairavi, Anandabhairavi, Kambhoji, Sankarabharanam* and *Kalyani* and in rare *Ragas* like *Manji* and *Chintamani.*

He was also the architect of the musical form called *Svarajati,* which was originally a dance form converted into an attractive musical form. His control over *Laya* and *Tala* was indeed exceptional and it is said that on one occasion, he rendered a *Pallavi* in *Sarabhanandha Tala,* which had 79 *Aksharas* to a cycle with intricate internal divisions. It is said that in a much inspired moment, during his journey to *Madurai,* with his *Shishya, Alasur Krishnayyar,* he completed nine *Kritis* in praise of Goddess *Meenakshi* and called them *Navaratnamalika.* Eversince, it became customary for his descendants to be received with Temple honours at the Shrine of the Goddess.

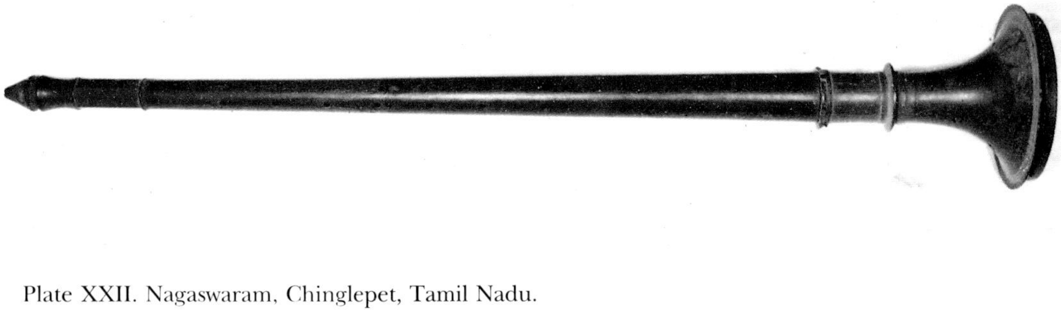

Plate XXII. Nagaswaram, Chinglepet, Tamil Nadu.

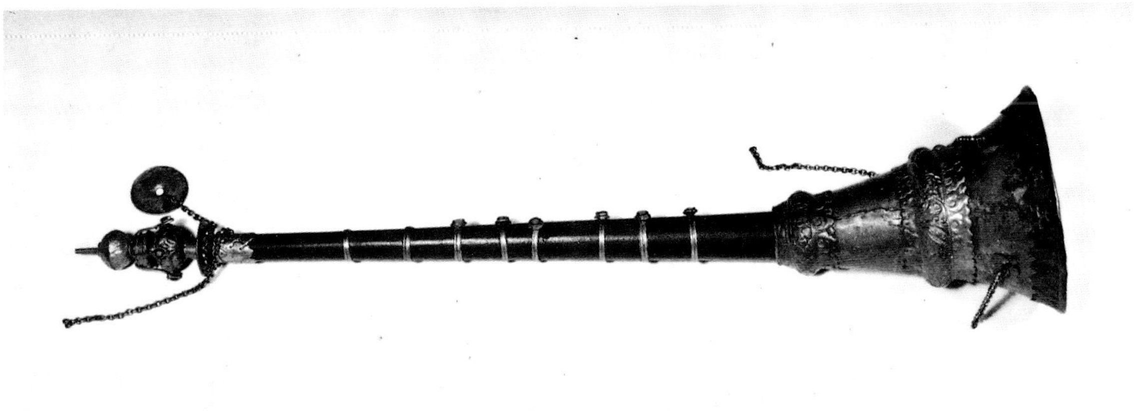

Plate XXIII. Shehnai, Kalimpong, East India.

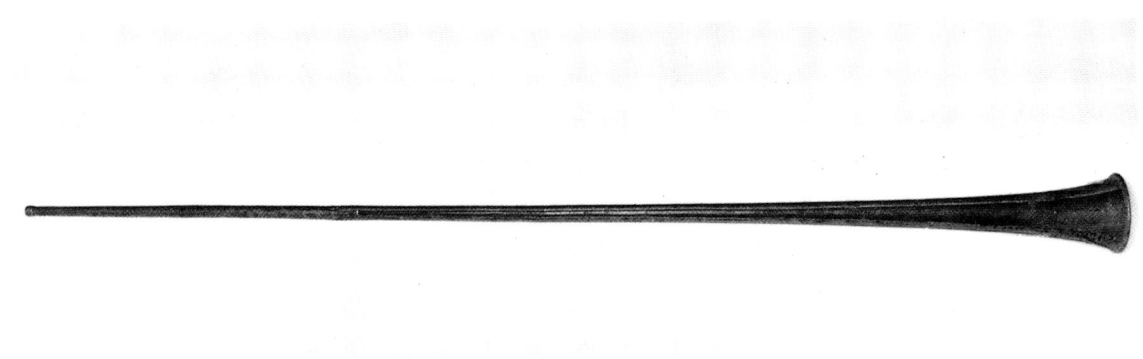

Plate XXIV. Long Horn.

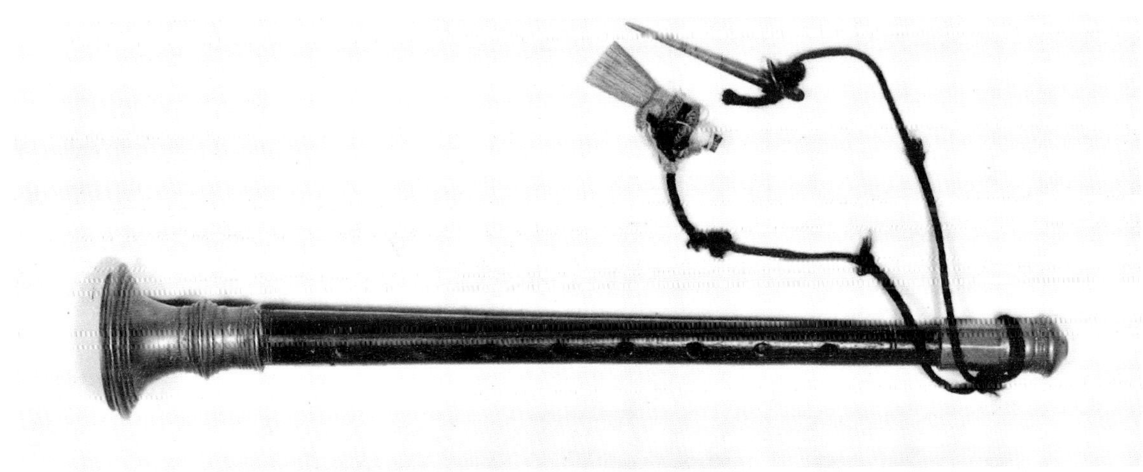

Plate XXV. Mukha Veena, Tamil Nadu, Played by the famous Mukha Veena Vidwan Late Shri Venugopal Reddi.

Plate XXVI. Organ, Calcutta.

The second jewel of the Musical Trinity, *Saint Tyagaraja,* has been immortalised by his *Pancharatna Kritis.* An author of both music and *Sahitya* (literature) or an *Uttama Vaggeyakara,* his compositions mostly emanated from him as a *Dhatu-Matu-karu* (one who is the author of both music and literature) during his inspired moments. His *Kritis* are noted for their musical content and beauty of language and presentation.

Apart from the *Pancharatna Kritis,* his *Utsava Sampraday Kirtanas* and *Divyanama Sankeertanas* which are renderd at devotional congregations, are famous as are the operas *Prahlad Bhakti Vijayam* and *Nauka Charitram.* While the majority of his compositions were in *Telugu, Karnatak Ragas* including *Karaharipriya, Harikamboji* and *Devagandhari* were infused with new dimensions and possibilities. Perhaps the supremely divine quality of his music emanated from his spiritual prowess and devotion to *Bhakti* as also his irrevocable faith in *Lord Rama.*

Plate XXVII.
Shruti Peti,
Lahore, Pakistan.

Plate XXVIII.
Harmonium,
Bombay.

Muthuswami Dikshitar, the third of the Musical Trinity, composed *Kritis* and *Raga Malikas*. A wanderer in search of spiritual bliss and a master in *Sanskrit* literature, famous are the *Tiruttani Kritis* that he composed in praise of *Lord Subramanya.* Later, while on a pilgrimage to *Kanchipuram,* presided over by *Goddess Kamakshi,* several masterpieces were composed by *Dikshitar* in praise of the Goddess. A scholar in *Vedantic* philosophy, his compositions are characterised by versatility, imagination and profundity of thought. In some of the rare *Ragas* including *Saranga*

Nata, Kumudakraiya and *Amritavarshini*, his compositions are perhaps among the few surviving references. *Dikshitar's* famous compositions include the *Tiruttani Kritis, Navavarna Kritis* and *Navagraha Kritis.* Two distinguishing features of his style are the doubling of tempo after the opening *Pallavi* and/or *Anupallavi*, wherein the text and music are arranged at twice the speed. The other novel feature is the *Vibhakti* or case inflection of words, whereby a phrase is so constructed that it can be split without any loss of meaning. A classic example of this is "*Tyagaraja Yoga Vaibhavam*" in *Raga Ananda Bhairavi.* A set of words is thus divided into sections such as *Raja Yoga Vaibhavam, Yoga Vaibhavam, Vaibhavam* and *Bhavam. Dikshitar's* versatility and broad-based compositions are evidenced by his *Kritis* in *Ragas* like *Brindavani Sarang, Hamir Kalyani* (similar to the *Hindustani Raga Kedar*) which contain suggestions of *Hindustani* music progressions.

Many royal personages adorn the pages of India's musical history and amongst them the position of *Swati Tirunal* (c. 1813-1847) is indeed unique. At once a versatile genius, a linguist, a gifted musician and composer in as many as six languages: *Sanskrit, Telugu, Malayalam, Marathi, Hindi* and *Urdu*, it was during his time that *Travancore* became an important centre for music. There were a galaxy of eminent musicians and composers in the Court of *Swati Tirunal.* The maturity and richness of his musical compositions are unravelled in his *Kritis* and *Varnas,* which with their majesty and grandeur leave a deep and indelible impression on the mind of the listener. Among his *Ragamalikas, Pannagendra Sayana* and the *Dasavtara Ragamalika* are famous. In the *Navaratnamalika, Nava-Vidha Bhakti* or the nine forms of *Bhakti* are manifested. The nine forms are (1) *Shravana* (Hearing); (2) *Kirtana* (Praying); (3) *Smarana* (Remembering); (4) *Padasevana* (Resorting to the feet); (5) *Archana* (Worship); (6) *Namaskar* (Bowing); (7) *Dasya* (Service); (8) *Sakhyatva* (Friendship); (9) *Atmanivedana* (Surrender of the Self). He also composed in *Hindustani Ragas* like *Bibas.* His *Varna Chalamela* in *Raga Sankharabharana—Adi Tala* is brilliant in musical setting and regarded as a model of perfection and is indeed a splendid testimony of the genius of the royal composer.

Parameswara Bhagwatar was a worthy companion of *Swati Tirunal,* while *Vadivelu,* a violinist, was specially gifted an ivory violin.

Thus, the lives and masterworks of great composers and musicians have incessantly provided a perennial charm and sustained interest to posterity. It is their unfathomable contribution that keeps pulsatingly alive a system of music while at the same time explaining and unravelling newer channels of musical expression.

CHAPTER VII

Musical Instruments Through the Ages

"Still must I like a homeless bird
Wander, foresaking all;
The earthly loves and worldly lures
That held my life in thrall
And follow, follow, answering
The magical flute-call."

—*"The Sceptred Flute"*
by Sarojini Naidu

Ever since prehistoric times, when humans discovered that agreeable sounds could be produced by striking pieces of wood, blowing through an animal horn or twanging the gut strings of their hunting bows, they have relentlessly sought to improve tonal quality by refining the tools—the instruments—that produce them. Therefore a study of the variety and stupendous range of musical instruments is not only fascinating and desirable but also essential for a proper appreciation of the various styles and forms that constitute the core and essence of the classical music tradition of India.

Scales and tunes are, by their very nature, rather nebulous, while actual auditory records of the music of ancient human groups in India, at least in certain areas, are somewhat elusive, thereby posing a challenge to many a researcher. Interestingly, a study of tribal and folk music has provided tangible evidence regarding the various facets of an ethnic group. Thus for instance, the wood used in a drum, the metal in which a cymbal has been cast, the hair of a bow etc., are all indicators of various geophysical features of a region.

Again, the migration of musical instruments could trace the wanderings of human society from one region to another.

Furthermore, since several of the Indian instruments are associated with Divinity, their study does provide valuable insight into the socio-religious customs of an ethnic group.

Interestingly, the characteristics of the individual instruments can be traced back to the oldest scriptures and treatises on music as also depictions in sculpture and painting and while there has been no appreciable modification of the instruments, over the centuries, the instruments have retained their distinctive character. In fact the remodelling and experimentation has resulted in contributing to the infinite variety of tonal sound and increasing the range of musical variety and possibilities.

Thus, while it is now widely accepted that the *Aryans* brought with them the *Venu* (flute) and *Vina* (harp) which were used extensively in the performance of *Vedic* rituals, the use of the *Yazh* was distinctly a facet of *Dravidian* culture. Similarly, some of the other instruments too have been contributed by numerous migrants.

This migration however has not entirely been a one-way movement. *Greater India* provides unequivocal evidence in this regard. A notable example is the *Ravanahasta Veena,* a bow instrument used in the western parts of India and is, according to certain scholars, a possible precursor of the *Violin.*

As for the range, there are at least five hundred known musical instruments, including those used in classical, folk and tribal music.

Regarding their classification, these instruments are generally of four kinds: *Tatya Vadya* (stringed instruments), *Sushira Vadya* (wind instruments), *Avannadha Vadya* (covered instruments or drums) and *Ghana Vadya* (solid instruments). The above classification broadly corresponds to the Western Chordophones, Aerophones, Membranophones and Idiophones.

TATYA VADYA—STRINGED INSTRUMENTS

Among the stringed instruments, the *Veena* has been described in the ancient texts for, perhaps, over a thousand years. Traditionally associated with *Saraswati* the *Goddess of Wisdom and Learning,* the *Eka tantri Veena* is extolled as the "original" *Veena* or *Brahma Veena* and the Goddess is said to reside in it. This instrument is played both in the North and South. *Veena* as played in the South is also sometimes known as the *Saraswati Veena.* The *Ekanda Veena* is considered to be of very high quality, having been carved out of a single log of wood. At the farther end of the finger-board and under it, is another gourd, which acts as a sound resonator. The frets of metal are broad and are fixed by means of wax. The strings are four in number and are tuned to *Sa, Pa, Sa, Pa* and pass over a wide bridge. The additional three drone strings, tuned to *Sa, Pa, Sa,* pass over an auxiliary metal bridge and serve both as a drone and for the purpose of giving *Tala.*

Somewhat similar in structure but without frets is the *Vichitra Veena* of North India and the *Gottuvadyam* of the South. Both, by way of construction and

Plate 15. Sorath Ragini, Malwa, Central India.

plucking, the former is similar to the *Rudra Been,* while the latter is almost like the *Saraswati Veena.*

Researches into history have revealed that the earliest instrument in this country was, perhaps, the *harp.* Bow-shaped, with a varying number of strings made of either fibre or gut, there was one string for each note which was plucked either by the fingers or with a plectrum called *Kona.* This was known by the generic term "*Veena*", with specific distinguishing names. The *Yazh* of the ancient *Tamil* region was also similar, descriptions of which exist in old *Tamil* works dating from the 2nd century A.D. onwards. The sculpture and murals of ancient times including the *Bharhut Stupa* (1st-2nd century B.C.) and the frescoes of *Ajanta* (2nd-3rd century A.D.) contain excellent representations of *Veenas* and *Yazhs.* While the structure of these ancient *Veenas* could have proved to be a handicap to the intricacies of glides, trills, frills and embellishments towards which the melodic content of Indian classical music was shifting perceptibly, but surely, newer trends in melodic enunciation necessitated the replacement of the harp-like *Veena* by finger-board instruments such as the modern *Veena, Sitar* and *Sarod.*

While the *Sitar* is similar to the *Veena* and was variously referred to as *Tritantri Veena, Chitra Veena* or *Parivadini, Amir Khusrau* (13th century) is said to have made certain alterations and also renamed it as *"Sehtar"* (*Persian* for "*three-stringed*") although there exists no documentary evidence in support of this. It is also contended that the *Sitar* is a modified version of the fretted lutes depicted in sculpture

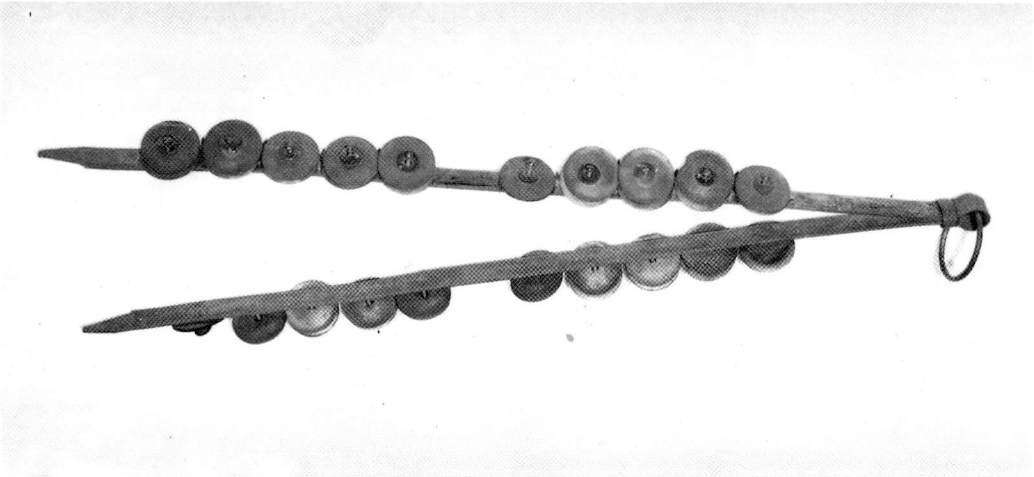

Plate XXIX. Chimta, North India.

Plate XXX. Manjira (cymbals). Bundelkhand, Madhya Pradesh.

from about the 12th century A.D. The *Sitar* is made of wood at the lower end of which is the *Thumba* (gourd), which is in fact a sound-box. From this projects a long finger-board which may often have a small gourd at the upper end, acting as an additional sound resonator. The frets on the finger-board are tied by guts at appropriate places in order to suit the notes and scale of a *Raga*. The five metallic strings pass over a bridge on the cover of the lower resonator and are generally tuned to *Ma, Sa, Pa, Sa, Pa* (*Fa, Doh, Sol, Doh, Sol*). There are two additional strings called *Chikari* tuned to *Sa* (*Doh*) and are extensively used in *Jhala*. The *Tarab* strings, usually 14 in number, are positioned below the main strings and are the sympathetic vibrators, required to be tuned to the notes of the *Raga* that is to be played. They extend from the smaller bridge placed on the lower resonator right along the finger-board, upto varying lengths. The extra sound generated from these strings enhances the resonance of the *Sitar* an instrument that is loved for its supremely fluid tonal elegance and timbre. It may also be mentioned that as *Khyal* gradually gained prominence, the *Sitar* came to replace the *Veena* in the North and has since remained one of the most popular stringed instruments in *Hindustani* music.

A cousin of the *Sitar* is the large, deep-toned *Surbahar*. It has a flat resonating gourd attached to one end and its strings are thick. These strings are tuned approximately five tones lower than the average *Sitar*. The essential drone instrument is the *Tambura* of the South and the *Tanpura* of the North. The function

Sawal-Jawab (Question and Answer).

of the *Tanpura* is to repeatedly resound the *tonic* note all through the composition, so as to intensify within the performer and listener an awareness of the basic note of the *Raga*. The contemporary *Tanpura* consists of a large *gourd* (or a wooden bowl, as in the South Indian variety), almost hemispherical in shape, acting as a resonator. The top of this is covered with a small neck to which is attached a long and hollow stem. On the flat surface of the resonator rests a wide bridge made of ivory, horn or wood. Over this pass four metal strings tuned to *Pancham* (or *Madhyam*), *Shadja, Shadja, Shadja.* The pair in the centre are set in the middle octave, the normal *Shadja* of the singer or instrumentalist, as the case may be. The *Pancham* or *Madhyam* and the last *Shadja* are in the lower register or *Mandra Sthayi.* A crucial though seemingly inconspicuous element is the thread under the wires of the bridge. This is called the *Jeewan* or *Jewari,* which when accurately positioned, lends the tone an extraordinary richness. In a deeper sense it is this primordial, pure sound that is evoked and communicated through the various *Leelas* of *Raga* and *Tala.*

The Thumba (Gourd). Sitar performance.

Another prominent stringed instrument is the *Sarod* which is believed to be a descendant of the *Rabab* of *Afghanistan*. This instrument is most often played with a plectrum of coconut shell or wood. *Sarod* is an instrument without frets and has a small deep body of wood projecting into a short neck and finger board. While the body is covered with parchment and the board with a steel plate, a small bowl of metal is screwed to the farther end of the finger-board. The melody strings are six in number tuned to *Ma, Sa, Pa, Sa, Pa, Sa* of the lower octave. These strings are plucked with the plectrum held in the right hand while the left hand is employed for pressing the strings on to the board. As in the case of *Sitar,* there are also the *Chikari* and *Tarabs* for resonance and emphasis on the structure of the given *Raga.*

Similar instruments appear in the frescoes of *Ajanta* (2nd-8th century A.D.) and the remains of the ancient *Buddhist* city, *Nagarjunakonda* (2nd century A.D.) and *Amravati* (1st century B.C. to 2nd century A.D.).

Another instrument of this family is the *Been,* which is relatively simple in construction, having two gourds, uncut and whole. These help in increasing the volume of sound. The bamboo or wooden tube fixed on the gourds bears a number of frets. Such fixed frets are in contrast to those in the *Sitar,* where they can be slid up or down, according to the notes and requirements of the *Raga. Been* is also associated with the *Dhrupad* style and the music played on it is heavy.

Of the string instruments played with a bow are the *Violin* and *Sarangi.* The place of the *Violin* a universal instrument of the world, both in the *Hindustani* and *Karnatak* systems, is indeed unique. Used both as an accompaniment as also for solo performances, it has an age-old tradition. In the *Karnatak* system, its place of prominence dates back to nearly two centuries and it has indeed become indispensable in concerts. Its challenge truly lies in the violinist's ability and dexterity in studying in depth its various traditional techniques, thereby enabling him to adapt this western instrument to the semi-tones and quarter tones of Indian classical music. The *Sarangi* is made out of wood, with the resonator being covered with skin and the finger-board with wood. The gut strings are three and are tuned to *Sa, Pa, Sa* in the lower octave. A set of *Tarab* pass below the main strings. *Sarangi* in the North is often used as *Geetanuga,* that is, accompaniment to singing, although it has also emerged as a solo instrument. Another popular bowed instrument in North India is the *Dilruba* while in *Bengal,* there is a similar instrument called *Esraj.*

SUSHIRA VADYA—WIND INSTRUMENTS

These instruments are so termed because sound is produced by the vibration of air columns. Being hollow tubes, with or without appendages, they are classified as *Sushira* (hollow) *Vadya* (instrument). This family includes a large number of flutes (the one held across the face) traditionally associated with *Lord Krishna,* a favourite theme in Indian art. It also includes the *Mukha Veena* family, consisting of the *Shehnai* in the *Hindustani* system and the *Nagaswaram* in *Karnatak.* While the *Shehnai* is believed to have been imported from the Middle East, with its original *Persian* name being *Surnai, Nagaswara* is mentioned in the *Telugu* poem, *Skanda Puranam, Srinatha's Kreedhabhiram* (14th century) and *Ahobala's Sangeeta Parijata* (17th century). Also, while these are viewed as auspicious instruments, often played at festivities, weddings and religious ceremonies, they are now increasingly heard in the concert hall as solo instruments.

Other wind instruments found almost in every part of the country are *Sankh* (conch) and trumpets like *Turahi, Narsing, Ekkalam, Kombu* (horn). Though these are not really used in sophisticated music, they have always formed an important part of religious processions and ceremonies. The *Sankh* is even a sacred symbol of *Lord Vishnu.*

Flute, which is one of the most universal instruments of the world, is most usually made of bamboo although it could also be made of red sandalwood, cane, ivory, ebonite, brass, silver and even gold.

Plate XXXIII. Khol, Bengal.

The *Sangitaratnakara* of *Sarangadeva* enumerates 18 kinds of flutes, according to the distances between the blow-hole and the first finger hole; the distances varying between 2.5 cms to 45 cms. The flute, traditionally associated with *Lord Krishna*, is the *Murali*, also sometimes called *Bansuri*. *Lord Krishna* playing the flute is a favourite theme in Indian art.

AVANNADHA VADYA—THE PERCUSSION FAMILY

Drums are instruments, hollow and generally covered with skin (*Avannadha*) and are extensively used as rhythmic accompaniments. The sacred symbolism of the *Damaru* of *Lord Shiva* is well known. Thus it is said that when the Lord was dancing in ecstasy on *Mount Kailash*, great sages gathered around the *Divine Dancer* and watched entranced! When the dance concluded, it is learnt that the sages prostrated at the feet of the Lord and begged that the *Knowledge of Sound* be accessible to the humans. Thereupon, the Lord took up the *Damaru* and played on it fourteen times, thus giving birth to the fourteen aphorisms of grammar which also constitute the basis of all music. In fact, percussion instruments truly have a language of their own, whereby each stroke is clearly defined and identifiable by a name or "*Bol*" which can in fact collectively be referred to as rhythmic syllables.

Of the multitude of drums, in the *Hindustani* system, the *Tabla* which consists of a pair of drums, with a range of about an octave, is by far the most popular.

Plate XXXI. Udduku, Tamil Nadu.

Plate XXXIV. Dholak, Delhi.

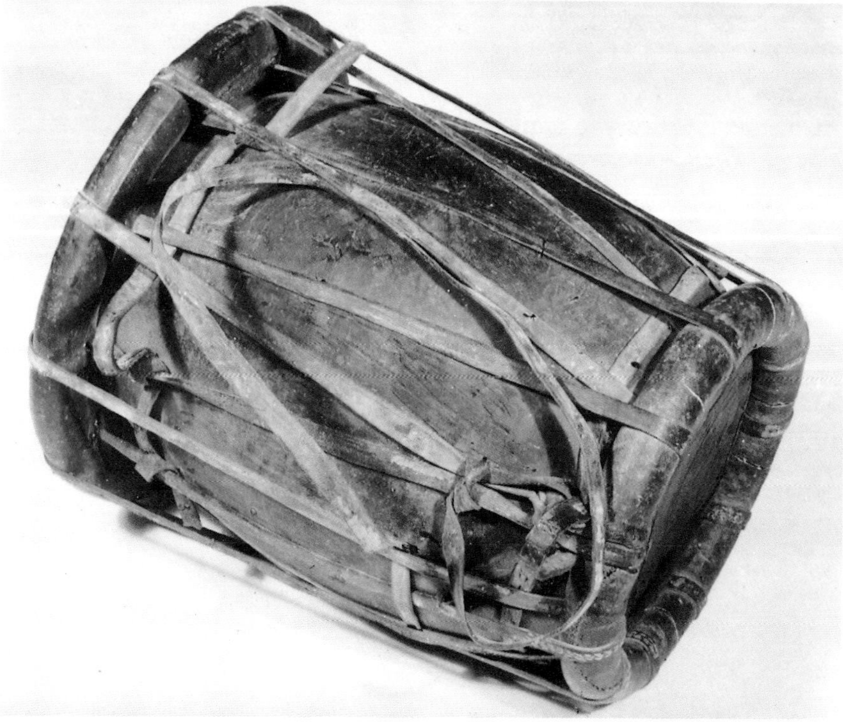

Plate XXXV. Dhol,
Chingleput, Tamil Nadu.

Plate XXXVI. Nagara (Folk), Delhi.

The duality in its appearance is amply reflected in the sound of the instrument . The *Dayan* played with the right hand has a light and quicksilver effect, while the *Bayan,* played with the left, has a heavier sound. *Tabla* is used primarily for *Khyal* and *Thumri* compositions as also for instrumental *Gats* (compositions for instruments based on improvisation techniques).

The *Pakhawaj* is the drum that was often preferred for accompanying the more heavy and serious *Dhrupad* and *Dhamar* styles of singing, as also instrumental music played on the *Been, Rabab* and *Sursingar.* It is a one-piece drum made of clay, with two faces or heads tuned to different pitches. Today it is usually made of wood.

In *Karnatak* music, the *Mridanga* is the premier percussion instrument used. Being amongst the most ancient of the drums in India's musical history, it is, in its present form, a barrel-shaped wooden body. The membrane forming the face of the drum is rather complex as it has a set of two or more suitably cut circular pieces which are stuck together. The two faces are held to the body by means of plaits and fastened to each other by a strap of leather passing through the plaits. Cylindrical wooden blocks (usually 8 in number) are placed below the plaits and are employed for tuning.

The *Manjira* or *Kanjira, Madal* or *Madhalan* and *Nagara* are among some of the other varieties of *Avannadha Vadya.*

GHANA VADYA

The idiophones, though perhaps among the earliest of instruments, have remained relatively undeveloped. In *Ghana Vadya,* there are essentially two instruments of considerable prominence. The *Ghatam,* an earthenware pot, without a skin covering, is capable of producing astounding sounds despite its humble exterior. While it is a folk instrument in some areas including Kashmir, where it is known as *Noot, Ghatam* is extensively used in the concerts of *Karnatak* music.

The *Jaltarang* is yet another important member of the *Ghana Vadya* family. It consists of a set of porcelain bowls of different sizes, filled with carefully measured, varying quantities of water. The size of the bowl and the quantity of water in it determine its pitch. Such water-filled bowls, one for each note, are arranged in a semi-circle; while the player sits in the centre of the semi-circle and plays on the bowls with a bamboo stick in each hand.

Before concluding this chapter, it would be essential to remember the fact that despite a multitude of musical instruments and their wide ranging repertoire, the ideal that every musical instrument strives to approximate, is the primary instrument or medium of music-making: "the human voice". The capacity of the human voice for communication—one of the most extraordinary aspects of our being—distinguishes us from all other creatures on earth. Through the ability to cause controlled changes of pitch—to sing—the voice could well be described as the most ancient, universal and sophisticated of all musical instruments. Singing is as old as the earliest civilised cultures. Thus, while the Aryans living in India before first century B.C. chanted *Mantras* and recited hymns while performing religious ceremonies, *Vedic* literature also contains references to musical instruments and the *Samagana.* The voice has no limitations. It is natural. It is also spontaneous and capable of echoing what is perceived by the ear. It can also portray the emotion and imagination of the singer. It is therefore at once indivisible, self-contained, inalienable and perhaps the most perfect example of a God-given gift!

CHAPTER VIII

The Garland of Ragas

"A picture is a voiceless poem,
*a poem a vocal picture."**

Any presentation on the elements of Indian classical music would be incomplete without a reference to the classic and unique form of painting, popularly known as *Ragamala* or The Garland of Ragas.

This unique form, at once direct, meaningful and evocative, indeed constitutes a confluence of two major artistic strands: *miniature painting* and *classical music.* It is the result of a merger and harmonious integration of several sources of inspiration. The *Ragamala* symbolises the codification of musical modes, the poems attached to each of them, describing its mood, setting and ambience as also the pictorial depiction of the poem.

Unique in the world of art, the *Ragamala* has proved, beyond doubt, the inter-penetrative nature of art forms, as eternal limpid melodies have been immortalized in a series of beautiful paintings. The instantaneous appeal of music and its ability to communicate directly and meaningfully has thus been portrayed by the depiction of the relationship of music with nature.

O.C. Gangoli, in his authoritative work, "*Ragas and Raginis*", has projected this dimension very succinctly thus: "*The practice of visualising musical compositions in pictorial forms is no more confined to India. During the last few years a few European artists have made attempts to set down famous masterpieces of music into visualised pictures. The "twenty-four Preludes" of Chopin have received pictorial interpretations by Robert Spies, an English artist. A few years earlier, Miss Pamela Colman Smith exhibited in London a series of pictorial drawings, interpreting famous musical pieces, which included Panderwski's "Chant du Voyage", Chopin's "Prelude No. 4", Cesar Franck's "Symphony", Schumann's "Kinder-scenen" and Debussy's "Granada", and other masterpieces.*"

In India, this distinctive and superbly original style of "seeing sound" as depicted in the *Ragamala* paintings has evolved over several centuries. All known surviving examples of this tradition of art were painted between the 16th and 19th

*Source unknown.

Plate 17. Raga Dipaka, Kangra, Pahari.

Plate 20. A Group of Eighteen Raginis. A folio of Shri Guru Granth Sahib, Kashmir.

centuries. The main centres of these unique visual manifestations, inspired by melodic compositions, were *Mewar, Bundi, Sirohi, Kotah, Marwar, Jaipur* and *Amber* in *Rajasthan, Kulu, Basohli* and *Kangra* in the *Pahari Region, Malwa* in *Central India,* the plains of the *Ganges* and the *Jamuna* and in the *Deccan.*

These paintings were created in albums containing, most often, thirty-six or forty-two folios, organized in a system of "families". Each "family" is headed by a (male) *Raga* and comprises five or six *Raginis* (wives), sometimes also several *Ragaputras* (sons) and *Ragaputris* (daughters) and wives of sons.

The thematic content of the *Ragamala* ranges from religious imagery, poetic symbolism, *Nayaka-Nayika* (love heroes and heroines as found in drama, poetry and dance), portrayal of *Krishna* the Divine lover, and the blending of themes with the local character of the flora, the fauna, landscape and seasons and even the time of the day, measured by Nature's clock—the Sun. The subtle transformation from darkness to light, the magical hours of dawn and dusk, are articulated visually, through a series of reflections of the artistic mind, on paper and parchment!

Further, each *Swara* and *Sruti* is associated with a particular colour, a certain hue, a temperament and a reigning deity. When related to the *Swaras* of the *Saptaka,* the *Shuddha* (natural or unaltered) *Swaras* are associated with the call of birds and animals. Thus with the cry of the peacock is associated the *Shadja,* while the *Rishaba* with that of the bull. The bleating of the goat is linked with the *Gandhara* while the *Madhyam* is associated with the heron's call. In spring, the cuckoo is believed to sing the *Pancham* while during the rains the frog croaks *Dhaivat,* and the *Nishad* is trumpeted by the elephant.

The *Ragamala* paintings thus establish a fusion between the visually perceived "natural" sounds of the environment and those portrayed by a musician through a medium, be it through the ingenuity of the human voice or the versatility of a instrumental musical piece.

For purposes of illustration, a few among the outstanding examples of the *Ragamala* paintings are described and illustrated in this chapter.

The *Raga Bhairava,* visualised as a form of *Lord Siva,* is virtually depicted in all known *Ragamala* albums. *Raga Bhairava,* the Lord of the *Ragas,* is believed to have emanated from the throat of *Lord Shiva.* Generally rendered prior to the emergence of dawn, for invoking vitality, the *Raga* personifies the rhythmic image of *Lord Shiva* in his *Bhairava* form. The 18th century painting of *Raga Bhairava* (*Kangra, Pahari,* Circa A.D. 1790) depicts *Lord Shiva* with the Trident and Nandi, the Bull, the two emblems of the Lord. Another pictorial masterpiece depicted is *Ragini Devagandhari* (*Kangra,* Circa A.D. 1790).

The *Raga Hindola* is a melody signifying the festivity and gaiety associated with the *Dol* (Swing) and *Sravan.* It is derived from *"Hindola"* used by a young couple enjoying the season. In the paintings, the centre figure, *Lord Krishna* or sometimes a king, is generally featured as the main personality, seated on a swing along with his consort and surrounded by damsels carrying musical instruments. The *Raga Hindola* (*Malwa, Central India,* Circa A.D. 1690) thus depicts *Lord Krishna* or a Prince seated on a swing, while several female attendants entertain him.

Another masterpiece depicts *Raga Hindola* and *Ragini Telangi* (*Deccan* or *Gwalior,* Circa A.D. 1850) Often rain is shown to signify the beginning of the cooler and more pleasant season of *Sravan.*

Yet another fine depiction is the *Raga Megha,* a melody symbolising the onset of aureal skies, clouds and rain. Initially personified by a deity of grey complexion, with four hands, it later came to be given the form of *Lord Krishna,* a heroic figure personifying love and joy! The *Raga Megha* (*Kangra, Pahari,* Circa A.D. 1790) is a classic portrayal of a joyous *Krishna* dancing amongst maidens and rejoicing the onset of the *Megha* (rain cloud). Another masterpiece is the *Megha Raga* (*Malwa, Central India,* A.D. 1680).

Plate XXXVII. Madal, Nepal.

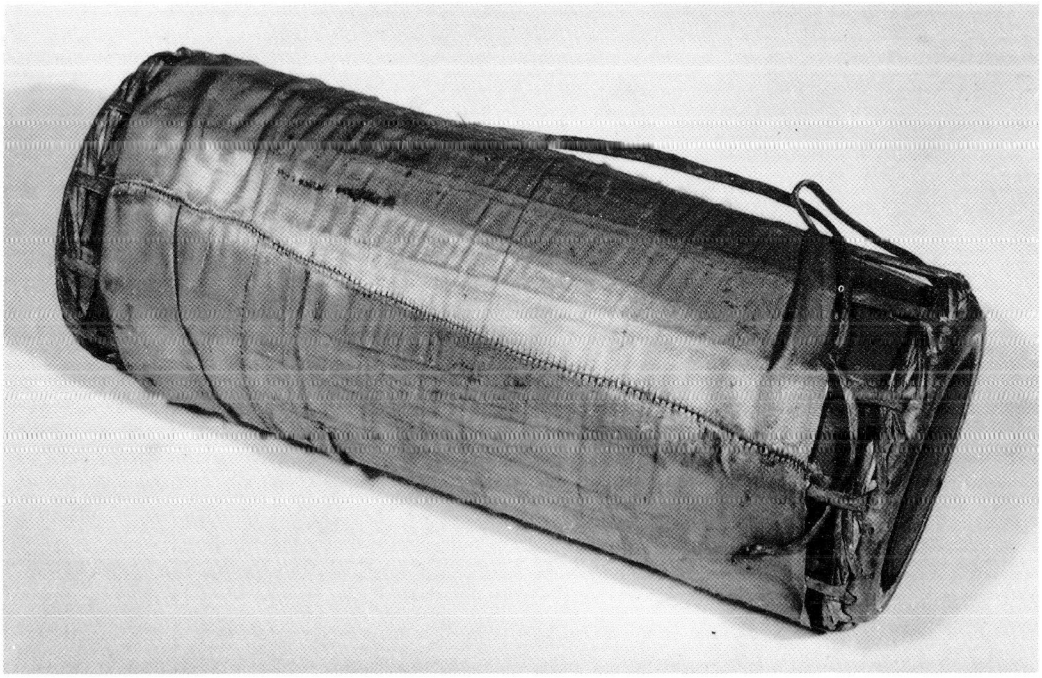

The *Sarang Ragaputra* (*Malwa, Central India,* Circa A.D. 1690) is yet another unique creation, depicting a prince playing an ingenious improvisation of the *Sarangi.*

The *Sorath Ragini* (*Malwa, Central India,* A.D. 1680) by the renowned artist *Madhodasa* portrays a garland making lady, while *Ragini Vasanta* (*Mewar, Rajasthan,* Circa A.D. 1700) depicts spring, a time for rejoicing after a cold and unrelenting winter.

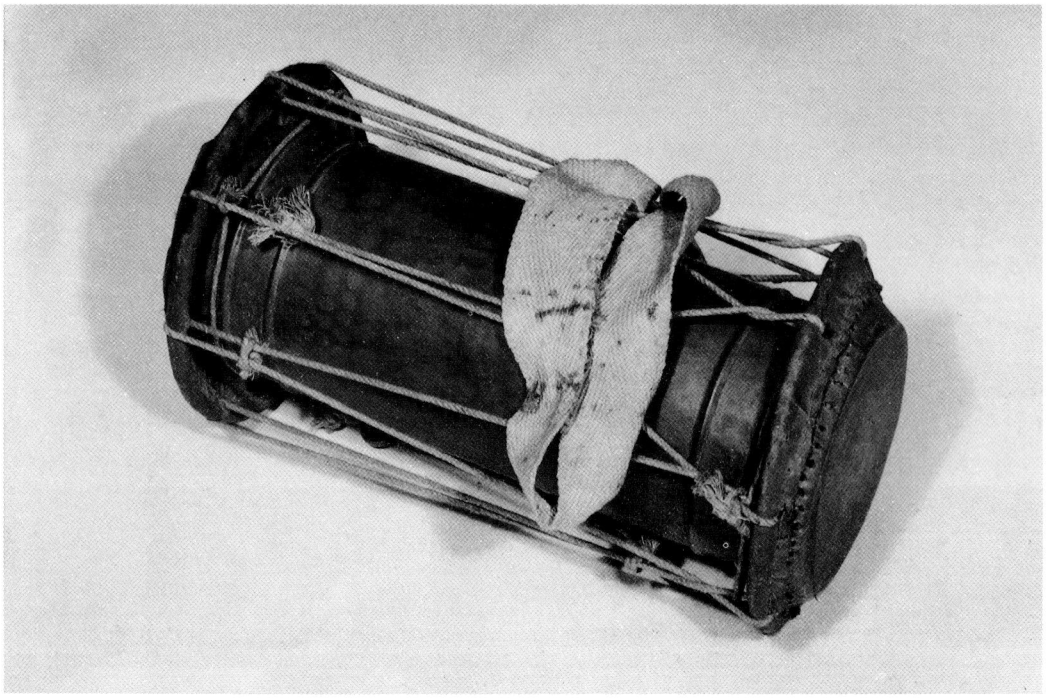

Plate XXXVIII. Pambai, Tamil Nadu.

An illustrative description of *Ragamala* would indeed be incomplete without the fiery *Raga Dipaka,* the almost unfathomable *Raga Malkaunsa* and the *Raga Sri.*

Dipaka, a *Raga* now rarely rendered, is deemed to have possessed the miraculous power of invoking light and heat. Said to have emanated from the eye of the Sun, *Dipakas* (lamps and fire), which symbolise the *Raga,* are invariably featured in the painting. A classic piece is the *Raga Dipaka* (*Kangra, Pahari,* Circa A.D. 1790).

The famous *Raga Sri* is named after *Goddess Lakshmi* (*Sri*) and was originally associated with the auspicious event of a good harvest and related festivities. However, later innovations came to symbolise good fortune. The artist has visualised the *Raga* by depicting the King and Queen listening with rapt attention and pleasure the music performed at the court. A fine example is the *Raga Sri* (*Mughal,* Circa A.D. 1620-25).

A *Raga* of almost unfathomable depth, which is generally performed after midnight, is the *Raga Malkaunsa.* The *Ragamala* painting of *Uniara, Rajasthan,* Circa A.D. 1770 truly personifies wealth, royal grandeur and youthful love. *Malkaunsa* is believed to have emanated from *Hari* (*Vishnu*) *Kanta.* Lotus, the emblem of *Lord Vishnu* and *Goddess Lakshmi,* is generally depicted to signify wealth, regality and love.

Plate XL. Dotara (Gourd and Leather), Jaisalmer, Rajasthan.

In conclusion, it may be stated that while the classical music of India is undoubtedly one amongst the various refined and sophisticated forms of artistic evolution that exist in the sub-continent, there are other numerous and diverse forms which are in reality a direct expression and manifestation of the cultural diversity and variety in terms of race, religion, language and other aspects of ethnicity. It is indeed a remarkable socio cultural phenomena that these manifestations and elements have through their inner resilience retained their identity and displayed an amazing elasticity and power of assimilation, despite the accelerated pace of acculturation, thereby proving the inner dynamism and the process of dialectical synthesis in our ancient art, culture and tradition.

Glossary

Abhang: Marathi religious songs, popularised by Eknath, Tukaram and Jnaneswar.

Adbhuta: Eighth of the *Nava Rasas* or Nine Sentiments, expressing anticipation and exhilaration.

Ahata Nada: "Struck" sound caused by physical impact and which is perceived through the ears.

Akshara: Syllable.

Alankar: A form of musical exercise.

Alap or Alapana: In certain styles, it constitutes the beginning of a musical composition which unfolds and delineates the essence and character of a *Raga*. Generally slow in tempo and with no measured rhythm, it lays emphasis on the *Shringara* and *Karuna Rasas*, portraying serenity and spirituality.

Anahata Nada: "Unstruck" sound or the metaphysical, unmanifested sound said to be caused by the vibration of ether, the purer air near Heaven. It is believed to be the sound of the Universe, experienced by the elevated beings.

Andolita: The sounding of more than one note at a time.

Anga: A tetrachord or literally a "limb" or "body" in Indian classical music. A scale consists of "Uttaranga" and "Purvanga".

Anudatta: "Unraised" sound. This is one of the two original notes in the early Vedic musical hymns.

Anuvadi: "Assonant". It could be any of the notes included in the *Raga*, other than the "Vadi" and the "Samvadi".

Arohana or Aroha: Ascending passage or motion in a *Raga*, usually applied to scales.

Arya: A melodious metre.

Ashram: A hermitage often in a forest, where a *Guru* (Teacher) and his *Shishyas* (Disciples) pursued austere lives under the protection of the *Guru* who provided guidance in disciplines including music and *Yoga*.

Ashtapadis: Songs which are 24 in number and are contained in the *Gita-Govinda*.

Audava: Group of five notes that may constitute a Pentatonic *Raga*.

Avarohana or Avaroha: Descending passage or motion in a *Raga*, usually applied to scales.

Baba: Literally means "Father". An affectionate expression used for one's *Guru*.

Bandish: A fixed musical composition bound by a rhythmic cycle.

Bayan: Left hand drum as in *Tabla*.

Bhajan: Hindu religious and devotional song.

Bhakti: Faith and devotion sometimes referred to as the Tenth Rasa or sentiment, combining feelings of peace, devotion, compassion and eventually God-realisation.

Bhayanaka: Sixth of the *Nava Rasas* denoting fear, awe and fright.

Bol: A drum stroke.

Brahma: Creator of the Universe and the first aspect of the Hindu Trinity.

Chakras: Centres of inner spiritual energy that evolved beings are able to activate.

Chalan: Description of the main features that characterise a *Raga.*

Cheesa: Fixed song composition.

Dadra: (i) Tala with six beats grouped as 3+3.

(ii) Light classical composition resembling the *Thumri* style.

Dayan: Right hand drum as in *Tabla.*

Dhaivata: Abbreviated as "Dha", it is the name of the sixth scale step of the seven-tone scale in ascending order.

Dhamar: (i) Cyclical rhythmic pattern with 14 beats grouped as 5+2+3+4.

(ii) A musical form originating from the folk songs of Mathura and Brindavan, the text of which is usually Brij Bhasa with the thematic content being the praise of Lord Krishna.

Dhol: A drum.

Dhrupad or Dhruvapad: Derived from " Dhruva"—"Fixed" and "Pad"—"Word", it is a grand musical style rendered in praise of God, kings, noblemen and nature. The style assumed glorious heights due to its adoption on a large scale by Miya Tansen.

Dhun: A tune often originating from folk music.

Drut: Fast.

Ek Tala: *Tala* with 12 beats grouped 4+4+2+2.

Gamaka: A grace note or embellishment used in Indian classical music essential for intensifying the melodic content.

Gandhara: Abbreviated as "Ga", it is the name of the third scale step of the seven-tone scale in the ascending order.

Gat: A fixed instrumental musical composition in any *Tala* or tempo accompanied by *Tabla.*

Gharana: "Family tradition" or a school of musical culture. Each *Gharana* has its own distinctive characteristics in the manner of musical presentation.

Ghazal: Romantic and popular song derived from the *Urdu* poetic form. Usually light classical in nature, it comprises of couplets and verse that could be secular, mystical or philosophic in essence and character.

Gita-Govinda: A Sanskrit poem which is at once a musical as also a literary masterpiece written by Jaya Deva (Circa 12th-13th Century A.D.). It inspired painting, music, dance, mystic adoration and is a classic and unique manifestation of Vaishnavite devotion.

Guru: The spiritual guide, revered master, father-figure and preceptor.

Guru-Shishya Parampara: The age-old tradition of teacher and student relationship.

Hasya: The second of the *Nava Rasas* or Nine Sentiments, intended to express humour, comedy and laughter.

Jati: (i) Scale or melody type.

(ii) Any of the classes/categories of *Ragas*, whose distinction is determinable by the number of notes contained in the ascending and descending scales. A *Raga* with five notes is "Audava" or Pentatonic. A *Raga* with six notes is "Shadava" or Hexatonic. A *Raga* with seven notes is "Sampurna" or Heptatonic. There can also be *Ragas* of mixed *Jatis*.

Jawabi Sangat: Adoption by the *Tabla* player or drummer of the rhythmic pattern presented by the musician.

Jhala: (i) Literally means "web". It constitutes the third part of the *Raga* presentation in instrumental Hindustani music, following *Jor*.

(ii) It is also played at the conclusion of the "Gat" with an emphatic acceleration of tempo to a climax, wherein very fast yet intricate rhythms are produced by the performer in close coordination with the *Tabla*.

Jhaptal: A *Tala* of ten beats, grouped as 2+3+2+3 which is generally used to accompany *Khyal*, in Hindustani music.

Jhumra: A *Tala* with fourteen beats, grouped as 3+4+3+4.

Jor: The part immediately following the *Alap*, characterised by the introduction of a pulse or rhythm but conspicuous by the absence of a fixed time-measure.

Jugalbandi: A dialogue or interplay between the instrumentalist and the drummer.

Kaharwa: A *Tala* with eight beats grouped as 4+4.

Kala Pramana: Temporal Ratio.

Kampita: A form of "Gamaka" or grace note, literally meaning "A shake".

Karuna: The third of the *Nava Rasas* or Nine Sentiments, reflecting pathos, loneliness and longing.

Khali: Constitutes the second of the two crucial points in a *tala* or fixed time-measure. It is the unstressed or "empty" beat often signified by the wave of the hand by the *Tabla* player, the other crucial point being the "Sam".

Khyal: Literally meaning "imagination" or "fancy", it is a richly ornamented and relatively less word-bound vocal style, consisting of two forms: *Bara Khyal* and *Chota Khyal*.

Komal: Literally meaning "Tender", where the *Shuddha* or 'Natural' notes are made 'Flat'.

Kriti: A popular vocal form of presentation in Karnatak music that is characterised by a remarkable emphasis on text. It is often a devotional song that provides a rich blend of text, melody and rhythm.

Kundalini: The divine and creative force that resides in its 'Chakra', at the root of the spine. According to the *Yoga* doctrine, at an advanced stage of spiritual development, this power when activated generates in the being complete control of the body and supreme enlightenment.

Larant Sangat: A form of dialogue or interplay between the instrumentalist and the drummer.

Lasya: The feminine dance attributed to Goddess Parvati, the consort of Lord Shiva. *Lasya* is regarded as the female counterpart of *Tandava.*

Meend: An embellishment used for the textural improvement of a musical presentation.

Melakarta: The classification of *Ragas* in the Karnatak system, based on 72 parent scales. The *Ragas* correspond to the prescribed scales.

Moorchana: The principle of shifting of the Tonic note or scale progressions, in descending motion, from the fundamental notes.

Nada: Sound.

Nada Brahma: The traditional intrinsic belief that sound is God.

Nava Rasas: The Nine Sentiments which constitute an essential and integral element of the performing arts in India, be it music, dance or drama. Each artistic creation is generally dominated by at least one of these sentiments.

Pada: A love song in Karnatak music.

Pakad: A short musical section that contains the essential distinguishing features that typify a particular *Raga.*

Panchama: Abbreviated as "Pa", it is the fifth scale step of the seven-tone scale in the ascending order.

Prana: It is the 'Soul' or 'Spirit' which the musician is required to infuse into the notes of a *Raga* in order to make them come to life.

Qawali: A Muslim devotional song.

Ragam-Tanam-Pallavi: The form of musical compositions in Karnatak music, usually constituting the main item in a recital or *Kacheri.*

Rasa: A sentiment or emotion.

Raudra: The fourth of the *Nava Rasas* or Nine Sentiments, depicting fury, rage and anger.

Rishaba: Abbreviated as "Ri" or "Re", it is the second scale step of the seven-tone scale in the ascending order.

Rupak Tala: A *Tala* with seven beats, grouped as 3+2+2 which is often played as accompaniment for *Khyal.*

Sadhana: Undeterred concentration and dedication essential for musical training and practice.

Sadra: A medium fast song in *Dhrupad* style.

Sam: The 'Stressed' beat or the most crucial point, sometimes termed as the centre of gravity in the rhythmic cycle of *tala.*

Samagana: The chants of the *Samaveda,* collectively referred to as *Samagana* believed to be the root of Indian classical music. Dealt with in the *Naradishiksha* (first century) and other treatises.

Saman: Music used for singing the hymns of the *Samaveda.*

Samvadi: The note or *Swara* in a *Raga* which is generally at an interval of a fourth or fifth from the 'Vadi' and which augments and strengthens the power of expression of the 'Vadi'.

Sangeet: A complex connotation signifying the union of the three elements of *Gita, Vadya* and *Nritya*; or song, percussion and dance.

Sangeet Shastra: The collective term for *Gita, Vadya* and *Nritya*; or song, percussion and dancing.

Saptaka: Seven notes (*Shuddha Swaras*) of the octave: Sa, Ri, Ga, Ma, Pa, Dha, Ni. Each *Saptaka* is divided into twenty-two *Srutis*.

Sari: A Bengali folk tune.

Sath Sangat: Interplay between the main instrument or the singer and the *Tabla*. Within the shortest possible time interval, the rhythm pattern of the main instrument is imitated by the *Tabla* almost simultaneously.

Shadja: Abbreviated to 'Sa', or Tonic note, it is the base note in a *Raga*.

Shanta: The ninth of the *Nava Rasas* or Nine Sentiments, which reflects inner peace, tranquillity and contentment.

Shiva: The third aspect of the *Trimurti* or Hindu Trinity, often represented as the Cosmic Dancer, *Maheshvara*, the great god, believed to have created music, dance and drama.

Shringara: The first of the *Nava Rasas* or Nine Sentiments, representing the romantic feelings of love and longing as also sensitivity to the beauty of nature.

Shuddha: Literally means 'Pure', it denotes the seven 'Natural' notes of a *Saptaka*.

Sruti: These are the microtones: the twenty-two intervals used within the *Saptaka*. An aggregate of *Srutis* constitute a *Swara* or note.

Svarita: Name of the first scale step, which later came to be added to the two notes 'Udatta' and 'Anudatta' in Vedic hymns.

Swara: (i) Note or musical sound which is the aggregate of a number of *Srutis*.

(ii) Tone of a definite pitch.

Swaroop: A short section of a particular *raga* that embodies its characteristic recognizable features (forms) distinguishing it from all other *ragas*.

Tala: An organised time-measure or rhythmic cyclical pattern, composed of various 'Matras' or units, constituting an essential element of time and rhythm in Indian music.

Tan: Musical phrases that can be sung or played in any tempo.

Tandava: The Cosmic Dance of Lord Shiva, symbolising energy, dynamism and the everlasting rhythm of life-and-death in the Universe.

Tappa: A vocal style that originated in the folk-songs of Punjabi Muslim camel drivers and later came to be developed into a classical form by Mian Shori. The texts are love lyrics.

Tarab: The sympathetic strings on a *Sitar* and some other string instruments, that are generally intended to increase the resonance and tonal quality.

Tarana: A song style in fast tempo, consisting of mnemonic syllables, instead of regular words.

Teen Tala: Sixteen beats, grouped as 4+4+4+4, which is a popularly used rhythmic pattern in Hindustani music.

Thata: The system of classification of Hindustani *Ragas* refined considerably by Vishnu Narayana Bhatkande (1860-1936) of Bombay. He distinguished ten *Thatas*.

Theka: Basic Mnemonic sound syllables or 'Bol' to form rhythmic phrases used by the drummer while playing a *Tala*.

Thumri: A light melodic, semi-classical form that could be either vocal or instrumental in presentation. The texts are romantic in content and express sadness and longing for *Lord Krishna* or an absent lover.

Tillana: The counterpart of *Tarana* in Karnatak music.

Tiripa: Stressing one note of a phrase. A form of embellishment.

Tonic: The fundamental note used in music or the main note of a *Raga* or its tonal centre.

Udatta: The 'raised' note, used in early Vedic hymns.

Vadi: Apart from the base note, *Vadi* is the predominant note that infuses into the *Raga* a particular mood. It expresses the *Rasa* of a *Raga*.

Veda: Book of the sacred scriptures of the Hindus, supposed to have been revealed by the Godhead. The four *Vedas* are the *Rig Veda*, *Sama Veda*, *Yajur Veda* and the *Atharva Veda*.

Veera: The fifth of the *Nava Rasas* or the Nine Sentiments, *Veera* expresses valour, glory, courage and dignity.

Vibhatsa: This is the seventh of the *Nava Rasas* or Nine Sentiments, expressing disgust, hatred and hostility.

Vilambit: Slow.

Vinaya: Humility. The attitude of the student towards the *Guru*.

Vishnu: Preserver and Sustainer of the Universe, Lord Vishnu is the second aspect of the Hindu Trinity.

Vivadi: Any dissonant note outside the ambit of the given scale, figuratively designated as "enemy" notes.

Select Bibliography

Ashton, R. (ed.), Music: East and West, Indian Council for Cultural Relations, 1966

Atiya Begum Fyzee-Rahaman; The Music of India, London, Luzac and Co., 1926

Bagchee, Sandeep, Nad: Understanding Raga Music, Eeshwar, Mumbai, 1998

Bhatkande, V.N., Hindustani Sangeet Padhati, Kramik Pustak Malika, Volumes 1-6, Sangeet Karyalaya, Hathras (varions editions)

Bhattacharya, A., A Treatise on Ancient Hindu Music, Calcutta, K.P. Bagchi and Co., 1978

Chaitanya Deva, B., An Introduction to Indian Music, Publications Division, Government of India, 1973

Chaitanya Deva, B., Musical Instrtuments of India: Their History and Development, Firma KLM, Calcutta, 1978

Dallapiccola, A.L. and Enrico Isacco (eds.), Krishna, The Divine Lover, Lausanne, 1982

Danielou, Alain, An Introduction to the Study of Musical Scales, India Society, London, 1954

Danielou, Alain, Northern Indian Music, Halycon, London, 1954

Danielou, Alain, The Ragas of North Indian Music, Munshiram Manoharlal Publishers Pvt. Ltd., Delhi, 2nd Indian Edition, 1991

Ebeling, Klaus, Ragamala Painting, Basel, 1973

Falk, Toby and Mildred Archer, Indian Miniatures in the India Office Library, Oxford, London and Delhi, 1981

Gangoli, O.C., Ragas and Raginis—A Pictorial and Iconographic Study of Indian Musical Modes based on Original Sources, Calcutta, 1935

Jairazbhoy, N.A., The Ragas of North Indian Music, Their Structure and Evolution, Faber and Faber, 1971

Jones, Sir William, On the Musical Modes of the Hindus

Jones, W. and N.A. Willard, Music of India, Sushil Gupta, Calcutta, Reprint 1962

Kamath, M.V. and V.B. Kher, Sai Baba of Shirdi, A Unique Saint, Jain Publishing House, 1992

Karnani, Chetan, Listening to Hindustani Music, Sangam Books, Orient and Longmans, Bombay, 1976

Kaufmann, W., The Ragas of North India, Oxford and IBH, 1968

Krishnaswamy, S., Musical Instrutments of India, Publications Division, Government of India, New Delhi, 1967

Manuel, Peter, Thumri in Historical and Stylistic Perspectives, motilal Banarsidass Publishers Pvt. Ltd., Delhi, 1989

Prajnananda, Swami, A History of Indian Music, Ramakrishna Vedanta Math, Calcutta, 1963

Prajnananda, Swami, A Historical Study of Indian Music, Anandadhara, Calcutta, 1965

Ranade, G.H., Hindustani Music: An Outline of its Physics and Aesthetics, Popular Prakashan, Bombay, 3rd Edition, 1971

Ratanjankar, S.N., Pandit Bhatkande, National Book Trust, 1967

Ravi Shankar, My Music, My Life, Vikas Publishing House Pvt. Ltd., 1978

Rosenthal, Ethen, The Story of Indian Music and its Instruments, William Reeves, London, 1928

Sambamurthy, P., History of Indian Music, The Indian Music Publishing House, Madras, 1960

Sambamurthy, P., Great Composers, The Indian Music Publishing House, Madras

Sambamurthy, P., Great Musicians, The Indian Music Publishing House, Madras

Sambamurthy, P., South Indian Music, Volumes I-VI, The Indian Music Publishing House, Madras

Sambamurthy, P., Syama Sastry and Other Famous Figures of South Indian Music, The Indian Music Publishing House, Madras

Sharma, Amal Das, Musicians of India: Past and Present, Naya Prokash, Calcutta, 1993

Slawek, Stephel, Sitar Technique in Nibaddha Forms, Motilal Banarsidass Publishers Pvt. Ltd., Delhi, 1987

Strangways, A.H. Fox, The Music of Hindostan, Oxford, 1914

Tagore, Rajah Sourindro Mohun, Six Principal Ragas (with a Brief View of Hindu Music) Calcutta, 1877

Tagore, Rajah Sourindro Mohun, The Seven Principal Musical Notes of the Hindus with their Presiding Deities, Calcutta, 1892

Van Der Meer Wim, Hindustani Music in the Twentieth Century, Allied Publishers, New Delhi, 1980

Wade, Bonnie C., Indian Music: The Classical Tradition, Manohar Publishers and Distributors, New Delhi, Reprint 1994

Select Discography

True musical appreciation begins with familiarity with the various musical styles, which in turn depends on extensive and perceptive experience.

Further, there are multiple recordings of musical works and compositions, rendered by different performing artistes.

Therefore, in order to maximise one's enjoyment of the great musical traditions inherited, personal prejudices should not be allowed to eclipse or dominate the selection of musical works.

The Select Discography is neither exhaustive nor prescriptive. It is at best an attempt to share one's own experiences in listening by identifying the various renderings of Indian musical art forms, both traditional and current, with a view to enhancing true appreciation and enjoyment of the nuances of Indian Classical Music.

Note: The variation in spellings of musical terms, from those used in the various chapters, is only to conform to their depiction in the literature appended to the recordings.

RECOMMENDED LISTENING

Hindustani Classical—Instrumental

Artiste	*Medium*	*Title*	*Salient Features*	*Label and Number*
Ali Akbar Khan & L. Subramaniam Accompanists: Zakir Hussain (Tabla) Ramnad V. Raghavan (Mridangam)	Sarod Violin	Ethereal Duet	Raga Jog Jugalbandi	Music India Cassette MC-A 5227 781
Allah Rakha Zakir Hussain Fazl Quraishi			Matt Tal Rupak Tal Sawari Tal Teen Tal	T-Series Cassette SICC 043

Artiste	*Medium*	*Title*	*Salient Features*	*Label and Number*
Allah Rakha & Zakir Hussain	Tabla	Drums of India —Ecstasy	Teen Tal (Punjabi Peshkar Qaida-Khard Jati & Gats) Pancham Sawari Roopak Tal	RPG CDNF 150067
Allauddin Khan Sahib	Sarod	All India Radio Archival Release	Masterworks of the Great Guru	T-Series CD SI CCD 095-099 (5 CDs)
Amjad Ali Khan A ccompanist: Rashid Mustafa Thirakwa (Tabla)	Sarod	Maestro's Choice	Raga Kamalshree and Raga Durga	Music Today Cassette A 91019
Amjad Ali Khan	Sarod	Morning Ragas Vol. 3	Raga Bilaskhani Todi	Music Today Cassette A 90003
Amjad Ali Khan Accompanist: Shafaat Ahmed Khan (Tabla)	Sarod	Afternoon Ragas Vol. 1	Raga Shuddha Sarang	Music Today Cassette A 90005
Amjad Ali Khan	Sarod	Morning Ragas -Vol. 2	Raga Mian Ki Todi	Music Today Cassette A 90002
Asad Ali Khan	Rudra Veena	Maestro's Choice	Raga Asavari	Music Today Cassette A 91012
Birju Maharaj— Vocal and Kathak & Zakir Hussain—Tabla		Rhythms in the Landscape	Tabla Solo Shiva Stuti Ghungroo Ki Uthan Thumri	CD Navras—Sony nād NR 00444
Bismillah Khan	Shehnai		Raga Shivranjani	Music Today Maestro's Choice Cassette A 91001
Hari Prasad Chaurasia Accompanist: Shubhankar Bannerjee (Tabla)	Flute	Maestro's Choice-II	Raga Durga Raga Bageshree	Music Today Cassette A 95004

Artiste	*Medium*	*Title*	*Salient Features*	*Label and Number*
Hari Prasad Chaurasia	Flute		Pahadi Dhun	Music Today Basant Bahar Vol. 4 Cassette A 91024
Baha-ud-din Dagar	Rudra Veena		Ragini Todi	Music Today Cassette A 97016
Hafiz Ali Khan Amjad Ali Khan Amaan Ali Bangash Ayaan Ali Bangash		The legendary lineage includes Rare Archival Recordings	Includes Ragas Bilaskhani Todi Yaman Kalyan (Recorded in late 1960s)	Navras CD Sony nād N 200812
Imrat Khan	Surbahar		Raga Mian Ki Malhar	Music Today Maestro's Choice Cassette A 91018
*V.G. Jog (Violin) **Hari Prasad Chaurasia (Flute) ***Nishat Khan (Sitar) ****Brijbhushan Kabra (Guitar)		Kalyan Ke Prakar	*Raga Shyam Kalyan **Raga Indira Kalyan ***Raga Yaman Kalyan ****Raga Shudh Kalyan	HMV Cassettes (2) STCS 04B 7745/46
N. Rajam (Violin) Accompanists: Sangeeta Shankar—Violin Ram Kumar Mishra—Tabla		Maestro's Choice	Raga Bageshree Kanhra Raga Jhinjhoti Dadra in Raga Bhairavi	Music Today Cassette A 91020
Ram Narayan	Sarangi		Raga Mishra Des	Music Today Maestro's Choice Cassette A 91009
Ravi Shankar	Sitar		Raga Asa Bhairav	Music Today Maestro's Choice Cassette A 91003
Shahid Parvez	Sitar		Raga Jhinjhoti Raga Kedar	Classics for Pleasure Cassette 05-026
Shiv Kumar Sharma Accompanist: Anindo Chatterjee (Tabla)	Santoor	Maestro's Choice-II	Raga Charukeshi	Music Today Cassette A 95005
Shiv Kumar Sharma	Santoor		Raga Kirvani	Music Today Maestro's Choice Cassette A 91010

Artiste	*Medium*	*Title*	*Salient Features*	*Label and Number*
Vilayat Khan Accompanist: Sabir Khan (Tabla)	Sitar	Maestro's Choice-II	Raga Sanjh Saravali Raga Mand Bhairav Raga Pilu Raga Rageshree Raga Gauti Raga Sughrai	Music Today Cassette A 95001
Vilayat Khan and Bismillah Khan Accompanists: Sabir Khan (Tabla) Nazim Hussain (Tabla) Basharat Hussain (Khurdak)		Eb'adat Part 1 Uphaar Part 2 (Live at the Barican Centre London)	Sitar and Shehnai Performance Ragini Yamani Raga Mishra Khamaj Raga Mishra Bhairavi	Navras Cassettes NR CC 0038 NR CC 0079
Zakir Hussain	Tabla	Maestro's Choice-II	Teental Ektal	Music Today Cassette A 95006
Zakir Hussain & Fazal Quraishi			Tala Pashto	Music Today Maestro's Choice Cassette A 91013

Hindustani Classical—Vocal

Artiste	*Title*	*Salient Features*	*Label and Number*
Amir Khan	Rare Archival Recordings	Ragas Yaman, Puriya, Hamsadhwani, Abhogi	Navras CD N 20091-2
Amir Khan		Ragas Hansadhwani and Malkauns	HMV Cassette STCS 850489
Amir Khan		Raga Chandni Kedar	HMV Cassette STCS 850190
Amir Khan		Raga Ahir Bhairav Raga Bageshree	HMV Cassette STCS 850478
Kishori Amonkar Accompanist: Balakrishna Iyer (Tabla)	Classical Encounters—A Live Experience with Gana Saraswati	Ragas Jaitshree and Dhavalshree	BMG CD 50578

Artiste	*Title*	*Salient Features*	*Label and Number*
Kishori Amonkar Accompanist: Balakrishna Iyer (Tabla)	Hindustani Vocal—Kishori Amonkar	Raga Rageshree	TIPS Cassette TC - 2508
Kishori Amonkar Accompanist: Pradip Dixit (Tabla)	Kishori Amonkar Excels	Raga Hansadhwani	BMG Crescendo CD 50892
Kishori Amonkar	Vocal—Rendered in Jaipur Style	Raga Sampoorna Malkauns	Music Today Maestro's Choice Cassette A 91006
Bade Ghulam Ali Khan (Volumes 1 to 11)	An All India Radio Archival Release	Featuring Masterpieces in various Ragas and Forms	T-Series SVCCD 113 to 123
Bade Ghulam Ali Khan	Thumri (Vocal) The Music of Love	Thumri	HMV Cassette STC 850179
*Hirabai Barodekar and Saraswati Rani **Nazakat Ali and Salamat Ali	Jugalbandi	*Raga Chandrakauns **Raga Abhogi Kanara	HMV Cassette STC 851266
Zahiruddin and Wasifuddin Dagar	Vocal	Raga Kambojhi	Music Today Maestro's Choice Cassette A 91011
Gundecha Brothers Accompanist: Srikant Mishra on Pakhawaj	Ancestral Voices	Dhrupad Vocal Recital Ragas Yaman and Charukeshi	CD Navras Sony-nād NR 01062
Gangubai Hangal (Vol. 1-2) Accompanist: Sheshagiri Hangal	Shakti and Peace—The Essence of Tradition	Raga Megh Malhar Raga Puriya Dhanashree Raga Bhimpalasi Raga Bhairavi	Nihad Cassette Premium NC 0022/23

Artiste	*Title*	*Salient Features*	*Label and Number*
Gangubai Hangal	Vocal —Kirana Style	Raga Bageshri	Music Today Maestro's Choice Cassette A 91005
Iqbal Bano	Vocal	Thumri in Mishra Tilak Kamod	Music Today Gulistan Vol. 4 Cassette B 91036
Jasraj Accompanist: Subhash Kamat (Tabla)	Evening Ragas Recorded Live	Raga Marwa	CD BMG Crescendo CD 50866
Jasraj Accompanist: Gobindo Bose (Tabla)	Golden Raaga Collection	Ragas Bihag, Basant	CD Times Music TDIC 002
Jasraj Accompanist: Kedar Pandit (Tabla)	The Essential Collection (Live Recording at the Queen Elizabeth Hall, London)	Raga Bihagda —Khyal Raga Gaud Giri Malhar —Khyal	Navras CD NR 00362
Jasraj Accompanist: Shubhankar Bannerjee (Tabla)	Classical Encounters	Ragas Hansadhwani and Jaijaiwanti	BMG Crescendo CD 50662
Jasraj Accompanist: Kedar Pandit (Tabla)	Maestro's Choice-II	Raga Bihag	Music Today Cassette A 95003
Jasraj		Raga Purba and Patdipki	Music Today Cassette A 97013
Bhimsen Joshi Accompanist: Bharat Kamat (Tabla)	Classical Encounters	Raga Marwa	BMG CD 50577

Artiste	*Title*	*Salient Features*	*Label and Number*
Bhimsen Joshi Accompanist: Shashikant Muley	Maestro's Choice-II	Raga Komal Rishabh Asavari Raga Bilawal Raga Basant Raga Nat Malhar	A 95002
Bhimsen Joshi		Raga Bageshwari Raga Hindolita Raga Jaijaiwanti	Music Today Cassette A 97011
Bhimsen Joshi	Vocal —Kirana Gharana	Raga Ramkali	Music Today Maestro's Choice Cassette A 91004
Mallikarjun Mansur	Vocal —Jaipur Style	Raga Nand	Music Today Evening Ragas, Vol. 2 Cassette A 90010
Mallikarjun Mansur	Vocal	Raga Shuddha Nat	Music Today Night Ragas Vol. 1 Cassette A 90013
Rajan and Sajan Mishra Accompanist: Sarju Sahai (Tabla)		Raga Desi Raga Shuddha Bhairavi Recorded at the Kufa Gallery, London	Navras CD Sony nād NR 00572
Rajan and Sajan Mishra	Vocal	Raga Jaijaiwanti	Music Today Night Ragas Vol. 3 Cassette A 90015
Padma Talwalkar	Vocal	Raga Jaunpuri	Music Today Morning Ragas Vol. 3 Cassette A 90003
Omkarnath Thakur	Pandit Omkarnath Thakur in Concert	Bada Khayal Chhota Khayal	Music India CDNF 054

Artiste	*Title*	*Salient Features*	*Label and Number*
C.R. Vyas Accompanist: Omkar Galwadia (Tabla)	The Essential Collection (Live Recording at Bhavan Centre, London)	Raga Mian Malhar —Khyal Raga Vasant —Khyal	Navras Sony nād CD NR 00542

Thematic Renderings

Artiste/Composer	*Title*	*Salient Features*	*Label and Number*
Morning Ragas Volumes 1-4		Refer Chapter VIII Contains both vocal and instrumental renderings	Music Today CD A 92072-75
Afternoon Ragas Volumes 1-4		Refer Chapter VIII Contains both vocal and instrumental renderings	Music Today Cassettes A 90005-8
Evening Ragas Volumes 1-4		Refer Chapter VIII Contains both vocal and instrumental renderings	Music Today Cassettes A 90009-12
Night Ragas Volumes 1-4		Refer Chapter VIII Contains both vocal and instrumental renderings	Music Today Cassettes A 90013-16
Megh Malhar Volumes 1-4		Refer Chapter VIII Contains both vocal and instrumental renderings	Music Today Cassettes A 91025-28
Basant Bahar Volumes 1-4		Refer Chapter VIII Contains both vocal and instrumental renderings	Music Today CD A 91021-24
Ras Rang —Evolution of Thumri (2 Volumes)		Renderings by renowned artistes in various Ragas	Navras Sony-nād NR 00812 NR 00822

Artiste/Composer	*Title*	*Salient Features*	*Label and Number*
Music Appreciation —A three part understanding of Hindustani Music		Volume 1 •Silence; Sound and Musical Sound; Voice and Instruments; •Swara and Raga; •Raga Sangeet Volume 2 •Articulation of Raga; •Raga in Performance; •Laya, Tala and Badhat Volume 3 •Forms of Music (Dhrupad, Khayal and Thumri); •Gharanas and Styles; •Music and Nature; •Listening to Music	Music Today Cassettes A 92017-19
Romantic Raga (Volumes I, II)	Romantic Raga	Refer Chapters III & VII Rendered by various artistes on —Shehnai —Sitar —Santoor —Guitar —Flute	Music Today Cassettes A 94009 A 94010
Asha Bhosle —Vocal Ali Akbar Khan —Sarod	Legacy; 16th-18th Century Music of India, presented by Ali Akbar Khan	Refer Chapter V Various forms of music including Sadra; Tarana; Khayal; Dhrupad	Music Today Cassette L 96014
Composed by Shiv Kumar Sharma	The Elements —Water		Music Today Cassette M 95010
Composed by Hari Prasad Chaurasia	The Elements —Wind		Music Today Cassette M 95008

Artiste/Composer	*Title*	*Salient Features*	*Label and Number*
Nusrat Fateh Ali Khan Volumes 1, 2, 3, 4 (Vocal)	Traditional Sufi Qawwalis (Live at the Kufa Gallery, London)	Traditional Sufi Qawwalis rendered in various Ragas including Ragas Bhairavi, Bilawal, Bhopali, Yaman Kalyan, Bahar, Mishra Khamaj. Traditional Qawwali in Hindi by Hazrat Amir Khusrau. Qawwali in Farsi by Hazrat Amir Khusrau. Qawwali in Punjabi by Baba Buleh Shah in Ragas Tilang & Khamaj. Ghazal in Raga Kedar	Navras Sony nād Cassettes NR 0016 4 NR 0017 4 NR 0028 4 NR 0029 4
Bhimsen Joshi (Vocal)	Sukh Anupam	Marathi Abhang (Refer Chapter I)	HMV Cassette SPHOS 45185
Bhimsen Joshi Volume 2		Marathi Abhang	HMV Cassette SPHOS 45090
Bhimsen Joshi Volume 3		Marathi Abhang	HMV Cassette SPHO 845071
Muzaffar Ali —Composer Rendered by Chhaya Ganguli Iqbal Siddiqi Zareena Begum Rolly Saran Naved Siddiqui	Husn-e-Jaana —The Beauty of My Beloved	The music draws inspiration from the traditions and lyrics of the 13th century to late 18th century Poets. Lyrics by Mir Taqi Mir Nazir Akbarabadi Quli Qutub Shah Amir Khusrau	Music Today Cassette B 97028
Song of Nature —Instrumental (5 CDs) Artistes: Ronu Majumdar	1. Babbling Brooks 2. Twilight Tunes 3. Dancing Daffodils 4. Flame of the	Music Inspired by Nature	Magnasound CD D4 H1 1701 D1 G1 0454 D4 H1 0678

Artiste/Composer	*Title*	*Salient Features*	*Label and Number*
(Flute) Vishwa Mohan Bhatt (Guitar) Tarun Bhattacharya (Santoor) Abhijit Banerjee (Tabla) Vilas Pednekar (Tanpura) Ronu Majumdar (Composer)	Forest 5. Beckoning Hills		D4 H1 0548 D4 HG 0701
Ecstasy Music: Sujan Sandhu		Soft Instrumentals for Tranquillity and Serenity	PAN Music Cassette PRM 5414
Serenity Composed and Arranged by Ulhas Bhagat		Soft Instrumentals for Tranquillity and Serenity	BMG Crescendo Cassette 40089
Music for Relaxation Composer: Vishwa Mohan Bhatt		Soft Instrumentals for Tranquillity and Serenity	Music Today Cassette M 94014
Music for Meditation Composer: Vanraj Bhatia		Soft Instrumentals for Meditation and Tranquillity	Music Today Cassette M 93026
Composed by Ananda Shankar	Shubh— The Auspicious	Contemporary Instrumental Global Music from India	HMV Cassette STHVS 854070
Ananda Shankar	We Remember Ananda Shankar and his Orchestra	Contemporary Instrumental Global Music from India	HMV Cassette STHVS 843199
Ronu Majumdar: Composer	Carrying Hope	A collection of works by distinguished Soloists, together	Music Today Cassette M 98004

Artiste/Composer	*Title*	*Salient Features*	*Label and Number*
Principal Soloists: N. Rajam (Violin) Vishwa Mohan Bhatt (Mohan Veena) Ronu Majumdar (Flute) Sangeeta Shankar (Violin) Baha-ud-din Dagar (Rudra Veena) Niladri Kumar (Sitar & Guitar) Atul Raninga (Keyboard) Rajesh Raj Bhatt (Tabla, Tabla tarang) Vocal Solos: Ashwini Bhide Deshpande and Kavita Krishnamurthy		drawing on both Indian and western modes	
Orchestral pieces Composed and Conducted by Dilip Roy	Namaskaar Melodies from India		HMV Cassette STHV 854055
Tanāv Composed by Raghunath Seth		Music for Relaxation —A Music Therapy —Soft Instrumentals based on Ragas Darbari, Shudh Kalyan, Bihag	BMG Crescendo Cassette Premium 50733
Music for Romance Composer: Louis Banks			Music Today Cassette M 94013
Music of the Deserts Composer: Zakir Hussain	Soundscapes		Music Today Cassette M 93030

Artiste/Composer	*Title*	*Salient Features*	*Label and Number*
Colours of Rajasthan Composer: Taufiq Qureshi			Music Today Cassette M 95021

Karnatak Classical—Instrumental

Artiste	*Title*	*Salient Features*	*Label and Number*
Chitti Babu —Veena	A Tribute to Chitti Babu (Carnatic Veena)		RPG CD CDNF 147844
Lalgudi G. Jayaraman —Violin Accompanists: G.J.R. Krishnan (Violin) Vellore Ramabharan (Mridangam)			EMI CDNF 147742
T.N. Krishnan —Violin Accompanists: Guruvayur Dorai Mridangam Vaikom R. Gopalakrishnan —Ghatam	Maestro's Choice	•Maha Ganapatim —Raga Nata Composer: Muthuswami Dikshitar •Mari Vere —Raga Ananda Bhairavi Composer: Syama Sastri •Raghuvamsa Sudha —Raga Kadana Kuduhalam Composer: Patnam Subramanya Iyer •Sarasaksha —Raga Pantuvarali Composer: Swati Tirunal •Parulanna Mata —Raga Kapi Composer: Dharmapuri Subbarayar •Ramarai Taruvoy	Music Today Cassette C 91017

Artiste	*Title*	*Salient Features*	*Label and Number*
		—Raga Sindhu Bhairavi Composer: Arunachala Kavi (Refer Chapter VI)	
Umayalapuram Sivaraman— Mridangam	Drums of India	Chatura Jaathi, Triputa Taal (Aadhi Taal) (Refer Chapter IV)	HMV Cassette 850689
Thala-Vadya Katchery —Conducted by T.H. Vinayak Ram		Instruments —Violin —Mridangam —Ganjeera —Ghatam —Muharsingh —Dolak (Refer Chapter IV)	Magnasound/OMI CD DSCI 5051
Kunnaikudi Vaidyanathan —Violin	Southern Strings —Instrumental Music from South India	Ragas Hansadhwani, Harikambhoji, Mohanam, Bilahari, Kanada, Nilambari, Misra Maund	HMV Cassette ST HVS 868438

Karnatak Classical—Vocal

Artiste	*Title*	*Salient Features*	*Label and Number*
M. Balamurali- krishna		Tyagaraja Kritis (Refer Chapter VI)	RPG CD CDNF 168329
M. Balamurali- krishna	Music of South India	Tyagaraja Kritis	Sangeetha CD KDV 039
M. Balamurali- krishna	Selections from Jayadeva's Geet Govinda	Ashtapadis from Jayadeva's Geet Govinda (Refer Chapter I)	Sangeetha CD KDV 084
M. Balamurali- krishna		Ragam-Thaanam- Pallavi	RPG CD CDNF 168376

Artiste	*Title*	*Salient Features*	*Label and Number*
Krithis on Vinayaka			Magnasound CD DSC V 5019
Purandara Das Krithis (Vocal)		Rendered by various Artistes (Refer Chapter VI)	CD KDV 025
Maharajapuram V. Santhanam Accompanists: Nagai Muralidharan (Violin) Thiruvarur Bhaktavatsalam (Mridangam)	Maestro's Choice		Music Today CDC 91016
M.S. Subbu-lakshmi CDs 1 to 5	Legends —M.S. Subbu-lakshmi the Supreme		RPG Music CDF 147202-6
Dr. L. Subra-maniam (Violin) Palghat T.S. Mani Iyer (Mridangam)	Dr. Semmangadi Srinivasa Iyer Evergreen Legends		AVM Audio CD 1069

List of Colour Illustrations

Plate 11
Raga Hindola and Ragini Telangi,
Deccan or Gwalior,
Circa A.D. 1850,
National Museum,
New Delhi.

Plate 12
Raga Megha,
Kangra, Pahari,
Circa A.D. 1790,
National Museum,
New Delhi.

Plate 13
Raga Megha,
Malwa,
Central India,
Circa A.D. 1680,
Artist: Madhodasa,
National Museum,
New Delhi.

Plate 14
Ragaputra Sarang,
Malwa, Central India,
Circa A.D. 1690,
National Museum,
New Delhi.

Plate 15
Sorath Ragini,
Malwa, Central India,
A.D. 1680,
Artist: Madhodasa,
National Museum,
New Delhi.

Plate 16
Ragini Vasanta,
Mewar, Rajasthan,
Circa A.D. 1700,
National Museum,
New Delhi.

Plate 17
Raga Dipaka,
Kangra, Pahari,
Circa A.D. 1790,
National Museum,
New Delhi.

Plate 18
Raga Sri,
Mughal,
Circa A.D. 1620-25,
National Museum,
New Delhi.

Plate 19
Raga Malkaunsa,
Uniara, Rajasthan,
Circa A.D. 1770,
National Museum,
New Delhi.

Plate 20
A Group of Eighteen Raginis,
A folio of Shri Guru Granth Sahib,
Kashmir,
Circa A.D. 1840,
National Museum,
New Delhi.

List of Black and White Illustrations

Plate XI
Sitar,
Rajasthan,
18th Century A.D.,
National Museum,
New Delhi.

Plate XII
Sur Singar, Bengal,
Late 18th Century A.D.,
National Museum,
New Delhi.

Plate XIII
Ravanahatha,
Rajasthan,
A.D. 1960,
National Museum,
New Delhi.

Plate XIV
Dilruba,
Uttar Pradesh,
Circa A.D. 1800,
National Museum,
New Delhi.

Plate XV
Sarangi,
Hyderabad, Andhra Pradesh,
Circa A.D. 1700,
National Museum,
New Delhi.

Plate XVI
Personal Rabab of Shri Jodha Bhatt,
Bengal,
Early 19th Century A.D.,
National Museum,
New Delhi.

Plate XVII
Santoor,
Kashmir,
1800 A.D.,
National Museum,
New Delhi.

Plate XVIII
Flute (silver, side-playing),
North India,
18th Century A.D.,
National Museum,
New Delhi.

Plate XIX
Flute (bamboo, side-playing),
Assam,
Circa A.D. 1960,
National Museum,
New Delhi.

Plate XX
Flute (bamboo, side-playing),
Maharashtra,
Circa A.D. 1975,
National Museum,
New Delhi.

Plate XXI
Flute (side-playing, ivory with silver covered ends),
Rajasthan,
Circa 1910 A.D.
National Museum,
New Delhi.

Plate XXII
Nagaswaram,
Chinglepet, Tamil Nadu,
Circa 1800 A.D.,
National Museum,
New Delhi.

Plate XXIII
Shehnai,
Kalimpong, East India,
Circa A.D. 1800,
National Museum,
New Delhi.

Plate XXXVI
Nagara (Folk),
Delhi,
1970 A.D.,
National Museum,
New Delhi.

Plate XXXVII
Madal,
Nepal,
Circa A.D. 1959,
National Museum,
New Delhi.

Plate XXXVIII
Pambai,
Tamil Nadu,
19th Century A.D.,
National Museum,
New Delhi.

Plate XXXIX
Ektara (Gourd and Bamboo),
West Bengal,
20th Century A.D.,
National Museum,
New Delhi.

Plate XL
Dotara (Gourd and Leather),
Jaisalmer, Rajasthan,
20th Century A.D.,
National Museum,
New Delhi.

Index